A *Conscientious* GUIDE
TO WARDROBE CARE

Easy Solutions. Eco-Friendly Results.

A CONSCIENTIOUS GUIDE TO WARDROBE CARE
Easy solutions. Eco-friendly results.

DEDICATION

I dedicate this book to my family, who inspire me to try to make this world a bit better. And especially to my husband, whose amazing eye for detail, composition and editing skills were invaluable in putting this book together.

I love you all.

Cover design by Jon Fraze

Printed in the U.S.A.

OUR PURPOSE

"We are in a time of increased awareness about caring for our planet. This includes being conscientious of the things we do that affect its well being, and taking doable actions to minimize our negative impact. With textile dumping in landfills becoming a global concern, the wardrobe purchases we make, how we care for them and dispose of them are an important part of what we can do, in some small way, to help the larger efforts of caring for the Earth.

This guide offers eco-friendly wardrobe care tips that you can integrate into your lifestyle; information that may help in buying decisions (to lessen clutter and overbuying); and some things to think about (as far as our perception of the wardrobe items we buy).

I hope you will find it helpful."

—Sheryll Fraze
(Author and Designer)

*"I say, beware of all enterprises that require new clothes,
and not rather a new wearer of clothes.'*

—*Henry David Thoreau*

Table of Contents

INTRODUCTION

We all love the excitement of shopping for a new outfit! Whether it is the latest seasonal trendy jacket, replacing a well worn pair of jeans, or doing a wardrobe revamp based on lifestyle changes. These are all great reasons to head to our favorite brick-and-mortar or online retailer.

What is not so exciting is what is happening behind our love of fashion. A review of recent statistics from the Environmental Protection Agency's (2018) data is enlightening. It is safe to predict that the figures are higher since that time, based on the trajectory. Even if they are lower, it is still startling.

- Landfills receive well over 11 million tons of clothing and textiles each year.
- In 2010, clothing and textile disposed to landfills each year amounted to approximately 8 million tons. In 2018 that figure had jumped to that over 11-million-ton figure. This means that there had been an over 3-million-ton increase in less than a decade.
- Only approximately 15% of textiles were recycled.
- Textiles can take years or decades to decompose in landfills.
- During the decomposition process, they contribute to the greenhouse effect, and leach toxic chemicals and dyes into the groundwater and soil.

It can be a letdown to see those numbers. To know that something we love and is an important part of our public identity could be contributing to an ecological disaster. This book is written to create awareness, yes. But it is also a call to action. To show that a simple rethink in the way we shop, maintain, and shift our clothing to another owner can make a difference!

By the way, you may notice that I use the word "shift" instead of "getting rid of" clothing. This is part of the effort to re-frame our language

around fashion. You "shift" something to another situation of importance, versus "get rid of," which creates a sense of it being devalued.
You'll also see that I use "inexpensive" (which connotes a price point
difference) vs. "cheap," which also carries that sense of being of
lesser value.

Let's face it, an item that is perceived of as having little value is
much easier to toss, right?

There is some bright news in spite of the dire numbers. Both businesses and consumers are increasingly aware of the ecological crisis
caused by clothing dumping. Some very important measures are
being taken to address the crisis. We have divided this book into four
main sections in order to look at the key issues involved in textile
dumping and ways in which we can offset the negative impact.

THE CONCERNS

This section covers a variety of factors that can cause clothing dumping. This ranges from buying habits and attitudes about purchases,
to environmental damages that can make items unwearable.

We also look at what happens once we have shifted our clothing out
of our closets, and how this can contribute to the ecological crisis.

A NEW APPROACH

This section details the Circular Fashion Economy: a growing move-
ment to respond to the ecological crisis of fashion dumping by keeping garments (and their components) in a continual cycle of use and
re-use for as long as possible. This ranges from sustainable manufacturing practices through post-wear alternatives that involve fabric
recycling and other innovative ideas.

THE SOLUTIONS

This section provides helpful ideas of how we can limit textile dumping. It includes wardrobe care practices that can greatly improve the lifespan of the fashions we buy. It also offers simple mindset changes around the clothing we buy that can reduce overbuying, and reset the perceived value in the things we buy.

TOOLS

This chapter contains tips and guides to make the task of wardrobe care easy to incorporate into busy lifestyles.

"You can have anything you want in life if you dress for it."

— Edith Head

PART 1 – THE CONCERNS

THE INFLUENCE OF FASHION

The fashion industry is a multi-trillion dollar business, employing millions of people around the globe. The industry includes textile mills, trim and accessory providers, clothing manufacturers, design houses, wholesalers and retailers. It is an important segment of the economy in many areas of the world, with locally-made accessories and clothing being a key source of income in some small communities.

There is, naturally, a push for the continued expansion of the fashion industry (and increased production levels) by those dependent on the industry for their livelihood and economic growth. While that is great for all us fashionistas, there is increasing concern about the ecological impact: particularly, the amount of clothing being manufactured; the constant chasing of fashion trends; and the practice of clothing being dumped to landfills once they are shifted out of our closets.

So, what are the main drivers for this increase in fashion production and consumer demand? If you are lured by the window displays of that trendy top you just saw on social media, know that there is an industry working in various levels to increase your likelihood of impulsively buying it. There are several contributors.

FAST FASHION

These "fresh-from-the-runway-to-you" companies can have the latest designer-show inspirations and street-style fashion trends on their store shelves in seemingly the blink of an eye. Rapid production and speed to consumers are their strong points. To be honest, how do you view fast fashion purchases? As long term investments? Or short term purchases that can be disposed of once the trend has passed? The latter is more likely the case.

These companies base their business model on constantly launching new collections. In order to do so and maintain attractive price points, they often rely on cost cutting techniques like using low quality materials and inferior garment construction. According to a recent article from Harper's Bazaar on the lower quality of fast fashion clothing, these quick-to-market garments reflect new trends but may not last through many wears and washes. These factors are seen as a major cause for the increase in clothing discarded to landfills.

RETAIL FASHION STORES

Traditional brick-and-mortar department stores once enjoyed the privilege of being the primary source for fashion. Not anymore.

They are now locked in a fierce game of keeping up with the competition. Those giving them a run for the money include fast fashion stores, designer brands who have both online and retail stores, e-commerce retailers, and even non-traditional retailers that are getting into the fashion game.

We have seen the trend of moderate and lower price mass market stores partnering with designers for limited edition collections. This has been an amazing opportunity for sales and for reaching a wider audience for both parties.

Faced with this type of competition, traditional brick-and-mortar department stores have gone from seasonal fashion offerings and sales to embrace the "fast fashion" approach: a constant influx of new merchandise and ongoing promotions to pique the interest of consumers. This revolving-door approach has had the effect of encouraging a closet full of clothing that may or may not enjoy a long wear cycle.

FASHION INFLUENCERS

These modern-day masters of selling have become a phenomenon!

What was once a loose association of individuals expressing their opinions and reviews on products and services has now become an organized, professional industry. Many fashion influencers have followers numbering in the millions. They are able to turn products into overnight "must-haves" and give brands credibility with their endorsement.

Authenticity is the key to their success. They are trusted by their base of followers, so it is important to them not to appear biased in their opinions.

Fashion companies have taken note of their potential and impact. Many of these influencers are now hired as Brand Ambassadors. They have become a powerful resource to sell fashions. They wear and review the latest styles for their brands and give encouragement to their base to try new items.

So what happens with the persuasive suggestions of trusted fashion influencers? We are likely to be more informed about the brand, the latest trends, and to have a yearning to buy what is new. Add this to promotional tie-ins and other "Buy Now" incentives, and we have yet another motivation to fill our closets with more lovely clothing and accessories.

Data has shown that we are buying 60% more clothing today than in the year 2000, with an average wear cycle of seven times before being discarded.

GLOBAL EFFECTS OF TEXTILE DUMPING

With the tempting promotional offers and lure of getting new clothing, most of us are sitting with a closet full of clothing. Some items are favorites that we wear on a regular basis. Some we pull out only occasionally. Some we don't wear at all (and may wonder why we bought them in the first place since the fit, color or styling may not work with our body type or needs).

Now it is time to de-clutter. But what to do with the unwanted items?

Let's say that donation is on the top of the list. This seems like a wonderful thing—giving clothing to charities that can resell them to support people and communities in need, right? Well, there are positives and negatives involved in this action.

THE TRUTH BEHIND DONATED CLOTHING

There may be an assumption that those unwanted dresses, shoes and other items that are donated to the local charity are automatically put out for sale, for a nice, long selling period. That may not be true.

- Garments are examined to make sure that they are in good condition. It also helps if they have "curb appeal," meaning they are a recognizable brand that will draw customers to buy.
- Oftentimes, garments that are donated may be so soiled, wrinkled or damaged that they are ineligible for resale. These unsalable items now become the responsibility of the charity for final disposition.
- The high volume of clothing being donated makes it easy for these organizations to be selective about what they sell.
- The charities operate much like traditional clothing stores. They also want to keep their merchandise on display looking fresh.

They will rotate stock out from the floor if it is not sold within a certain time period.

So what happens to merchandise that is damaged or has not sold? It is passed on to traders specializing in textile disposition. Some garments may make their way to fabric mills that can break them down to create new fabrics. Others end up with companies for use for post-consumer needs (furniture padding, etc.). A large percentage are packed into bales and shipped to the secondhand clothing market, mainly in developing countries.

WHAT HAPPENS TO USED CLOTHING AFTER REACHING DEVELOPING COUNTRIES?

According to SMART (the Secondary Materials And Recycles Textile organization), the second-hand clothing market supports the livelihood of hundreds of thousands of people in developing countries who work in trading, distribution, repairing, restyling, washing, etc.

While a certain percentage of this clothing meets with a positive fate, poor-quality and damaged items will eventually end up being thrown away to local landfills.

Whereas landfills in developed countries are equipped to process chemicals, poorer countries do not have the same level of infrastructure around landfills. Common issues that arise from decomposing clothes in these landfills include chemical seepage to local waterways, greenhouse gas emission and air pollution from landfill fires.

WHAT IS HAPPENING WITH DEVELOPING COUNTRIES WHO NOW OPPOSE TEXTILE DUMPING.

The used clothing trade represents an important profit center (totaling billions of dollars annually) for many developing countries. In spite of this gain, there are some countries who are now actively trying to reverse the influx of second-hand textiles. Why? There are several reasons.

- They have growing concerns about the damage from textile dumping on their country's ecosystem.
- As the world at large becomes more focused on sustainability and planet care, some do not want to be viewed as the voluntary dumping grounds for First World textile waste.
- They want to be viewed as innovative participants in the global fashion scene. This includes developing lucrative partnerships with other companies in the clothing production supply chain.
- They want to rebuild their own textile industry and export their own goods.
- They want to promote their own designers and brands on the international fashion stage. You can find countries like Nigeria and Lagos showcasing runway collections that follow the same International Fashion Week calendars as their Western counterparts.

According to a recent BBC report, member states of the East African Community, which comprises Burundi, Kenya, Rwanda, Tanzania and Uganda, announced they would ban second-hand imports starting in 2019 to protect their own clothing manufacturers. Some countries even have imposed tariffs on incoming used textiles, to further deter clothing dumping.

So, what does this mean for First World countries who have become accustomed to sending unwanted garments to developing countries? And what about those within these developing countries who have profited from used textiles? Economic pressures to preserve the status quo have been employed by those who benefit from the practice. It is an evolving situation beyond the scope of this book.

WARDROBE DAMAGE FROM PESTS

You pull out a favorite wool sweater that you have stored from last winter, only to be dismayed by a hole in it from insect damage. If you are lucky it is in an inconspicuous spot. Most likely it is front and center, which means that the sweater is unwearable for public appearances. Maybe it will be consigned to wearing around the house, at best, or tossed to the trash.

So, what attracts insects to clothing? Believe it or not it depends on the insect and the fabric. It should be noted that most pests are not in your house specifically in search of that silk blouse. They appear as part of a general infestation in environments that they find desirable (e.g. dark corners, places with humid temperatures, etc.). Your clothing provides them with nutrition they need while trying to breed and thrive in these settings.

Here is some interesting information from the U.C. Riverside Department of Entomology of common types of pests, and the reasons they create a nuisance for your wardrobe.

CLOTH MOTHS

Moths are what comes to mind when we think of clothing damage. There are actually a variety of them that are harmless, but the one that is particularly destructive to clothing is the Webbing Clothes Moth. This pest loves to hide out in dark places and can be evident by the silken webs spun by the larvae. The larva is actually the culprit that causes damage to clothing.

The female moths will lay their eggs in nutrient-rich fabrics that contain keratin. This a protein that is found in fabrics made from animal fibers (wool, mohair, feather, fur, alpaca, etc.). The larvae feed on the protein, by eating their way through the fiber and thus creating holes in the garment. Cloth moths are also attracted to other fabrics such as linen, cotton, silks and synthetics, if they are blended with animal fibers.

CARPET BEETLES

Much like the cloth moths, the larvae of this pest can cause damage to garments made from animal fibers. Unlike cloth moths, the eggs are not laid directly on the fabric. They are laid in dark places that are hidden from normal view and foot traffic. After they hatch, the larvae find their way to nutrients which they may find in cottons, silks and other fabrics.

It should also be noted that both cloth moths and carpet beetles will attack fabrics containing detritus of nutritional value. So, that slice of pizza, soda or juice you enjoyed are an attractive food source for these pests.

SILVERFISH

These easily recognizable insects have slender, scale-covered bodies that are sometimes silvery, usually with a metallic sheen.

There may be infestations almost anywhere in a house, including attics, wall voids, and sub-floor areas. They are mostly attracted to human foods on garments (such as crumbs and liquid spills) but they will also snack on starched cotton, linen and silk. The damage they leave on fabrics includes their discarded scales, droppings, or yellowish stains.

As a note, they seldom injure wool, hair, or other fibers that are of animal origin.

TERMITES, COCKROACHES AND CRICKETS

These insects are not commonly associated with clothing damage.

They are unable to digest keratin protein (the preferred meal for cloth moths), but nevertheless can cause damage by chewing through keratin-containing fabric. Wherever the infestation occurs, these fabric-damaging insects are potentially highly destructive.

On the good-news front, the use of synthetics for many woolen garments (plus insect repellent treatments at the manufacturing level) has reduced the over-all importance of this group as household pests. That being said, unprotected furniture and fabrics imported from other areas, without these protective measures, can increase the chances for causing damage to clothing and other fabric household items (such as curtains, tablecloths, etc).

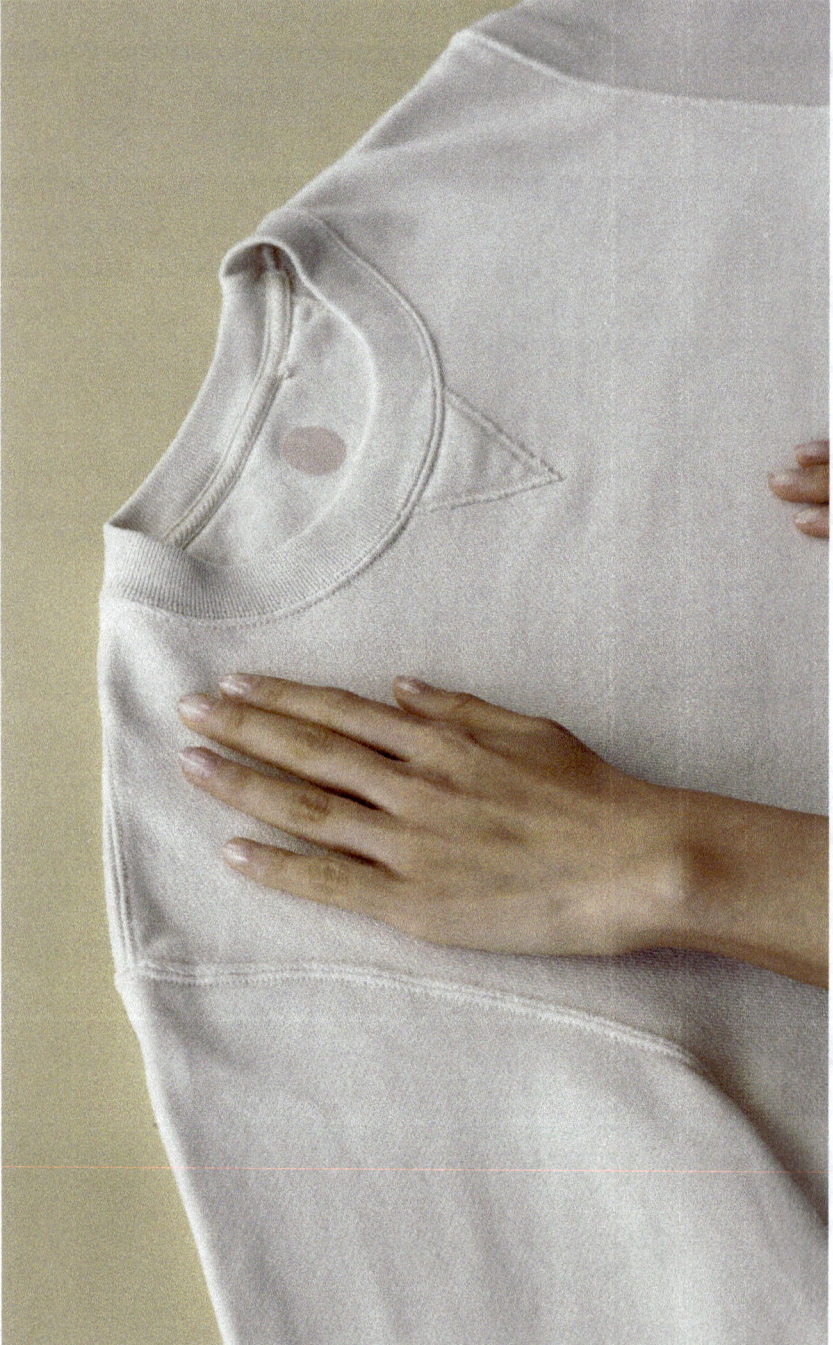

WARDROBE DAMAGE FROM NON-PEST CAUSES

Ever had a white top turn an unexpected shade of pink because a red one had accidentally been put in the wash with it? We've all experienced some kind of wardrobe misstep that put a favorite item at risk for being tossed to the trash.

The good thing is that some common damages that are not pest-related can be avoided with awareness and attentive care.

FADING FROM DIRECT SUNLIGHT

One of the few causes of clothing damage that is unavoidable is the effect of exposure to sunlight. Whether it is in the long days of summer or the shorter winter days, the ultraviolet radiation will slowly fade garments over time. This effect is less noticeable in lighter colors, of course. Also, polyester and polyester blends will not suffer this fate.

FADING FROM LAUNDERING

The two main culprits here are detergent ingredients and water temperature.

Detergent ingredients

Some laundry detergents contain bleach and other chemicals that are designed to dissolve tough stains. They are a wonderful thing for clothing used for rugged, outdoor activities. They are also fine for hardy fabrics such as cotton or denim. They might not be so great for that delicate silk or lace blouse. The harshness of the chemicals may contribute to colors fading.

Water temperature

Are you a "sort everything by color and water temperature" person, or do you pick an average "warm" temperature and hope for the best? Here is why it is important to pay attention to water temperature.

Hot water breaks down fibers and releases color more quickly than cold water. That is why washing brights in cold water is advised. In addition to temperature, your tap water probably contains magnesium, chlorine and calcium. These may cause fading to fabrics over time.

GARMENT STRETCHING

It goes without saying that some garments do just fine on a hanger and some are better stored flat to avoid stretched-out necklines and misshapen shoulders. That being said, most fold-able items do okay if the proper hanger is used: one that is padded and non-slip. It is also important to use a hanger that is appropriate for the weight of the garment (i.e. a heavy beaded gown stores better on a heavy duty padded hanger versus a thin velvet one).

In general, fold-able items may include garments prone to stretching such as:
- Sweaters with loose weave
- Beaded tops
- Garments made in organza, chiffon or other sheer fabrics

GARMENT SHRINKING

Finding a favorite sweater a size or two smaller once out of the wash is irritating. There are a number different causes for garments doing their version of downsizing.
- Laundering items in water that is too warm can cause fibers to compress and mesh together, thus creating the shrunken-sweater syndrome.

- Ever feel like those pants fit smaller if you wash them before wearing, after purchase? Well, it probably underwent varying degrees of pulling and tension during manufacturing. Some may even have special finishing. A wash before wearing for the first time agitates the fibers or removes the finishing. This lets the fibers return to their natural state (which can be smaller than the garment's original size before washing).

MILDEW

You know that musty odor that you can smell on clothing (often when they have been stored for a while)? That can signal the development of mildew.

Mildew is a form of mold, which is a fungus that thrives in moist environments. These are actually living organisms that travel from one area to another through air currents. Pretty much any access to your home can be an entry point for mildew. This includes vents, doors, windows, heating systems... and even on your person as you come in from the outdoors.

So how does it grow on clothing? Items stored in humid attics or bags that keep moisture trapped (like plastics) create a perfect setting for spores to settle as they move about in the air. Fabrics like cotton and wool are prime targets because they naturally retain moisture and provide nutrients for the mildew spores to thrive and grow.

If you have moldy clothes hanging in your closet, the spores can easily spread and settle in new locations such as on the carpet and walls of the closet.

STAINS FROM ACCIDENTAL SPILLS

It is inevitable that some wardrobe items will suffer stains from accidental spills. There are all kinds of methods and hacks for cleaning stains (we have included some in our resource guide). The best advice is to quickly handle the stains when they occur, and to be proactive in mitigating avoidable stains (e.g., using a face cover if wearing makeup when changing outfits to avoid lipstick smudges). These are some of the hardest stains to deal with:

- Hot Cocoa
- Blood
- Permanent Marker
- Tomato Sauce
- Grass Stains
- Red Wine
- Chocolate

CRACKING

A leather jacket or pants can make a striking fashion statement. The skin is supple, durable and will take on a wonderful "broken-in" look over time, with the proper care. But it is also susceptible to cracking. The main reason is humidity (or lack of it). Leather is porous, which means it absorbs and releases moisture depending on the humidity.

When leather is placed in a humid environment, the excess moisture vapor in the air will settle on the surface, be absorbed into the pores and keep the leather moist. Too much humidity can lead that wonderful leather garment to suffer the fate of other garments exposed to too much moisture: the development of mold and mildew.

On the other hand, when leather is placed in a dry environment, the moisture from its pores evaporates, thus making the leather drier.

If the air is too dry over a long period of time, this constant release of moisture will cause the leather to crack.

FIBER DETERIORATION

Most fabrics will suffer some deterioration over time due to wear and tear, exposure to the elements and other activities. The extent of deterioration depends on the construction of the fabric and its intended use. Fabrics used for mountain-climbing attire, for example, will have a high resistance to deterioration due to the rigors of that type of activity.

Proper care will offset some of the effects (i.e. using correct water temperature and techniques for cleaning).

STORAGE IN DRY CLEANING BAGS

You bring home your dress from the cleaners in a plastic bag, and it is very tempting (and convenient) to store it in that bag. Same goes for a fabulous vintage outfit. Having it in clear plastic makes it easy to spot and seemingly safe from pests.

The truth is that dry cleaning plastic bags are not designed for long-term storage. They are made cheaply from low-density polyethylene or LDPE, otherwise known as plastic film. They are okay as a temporary transport for your clothing from that dry cleaners to your home, but they will begin to disintegrate over time, releasing fumes that can weaken and damage fibers.

STORAGE IN HIGH GRADE PLASTIC BAGS

Using high grade plastic bags for long term storage is an improvement over using dry-cleaning bags. It is important to keep in mind, however, that plastic bags do not allow air to circulate within them. Trapped moisture and humidity creates the perfect setting for mold and mildew spores that may have settled on the garment to grow.

STORAGE IN CARDBOARD, WOOD OR PLASTIC BOXES
There are pros and cons to using these types of containers.

Unsealed wood contains acids that can migrate and stain items when in direct contact with them. The good news is: a barrier can be provided by wrapping items with acid-free materials tissue, blotter paper, washed cotton muslin, or old clean cotton sheets.

Cardboard boxes are not recommended. They can deteriorate over time and do not protect against water damage. Bugs can also eat through cardboard and get to the contents within the boxes.

Plastic bins seem a great alternative that stack nicely in storage areas. The same fate can happen to your prized garments as when storing them in plastic bags for the long haul. Even high-quality plastic bins can trap moisture in high humidity environments, and lead to mustiness and mold developing over time.

If using plastic storage boxes, the trick is to control the temperature in that area, to avoid extreme fluctuations between hot or cold. Remember that fibers do respond to the environment in which they are kept.

SNAGS AND RIPS
How exasperating to have a rip in your shirt, or yarn pull in a comfy sweater! It may seem beyond repair if the damage is major, but there are some ideas to salvage these wardrobe must-haves.

- Have your repair supplies ready to easily handle fashion emergencies. We have a suggested list in the Tools chapter.

- Up-cycle the clothing item by modifying it around the tear. For example, a rip in the sleeve of a long sleeve shirt can be cut off to become your new short sleeve favorite.
- When storing garments, make sure that more delicate items are together and away from items that have buckles and other trims that can snag.
- Protect garments most susceptible to snagging (lace, chiffon, etc.) in breathable, cotton bags.

THE ECOLOGICAL IMPACT OF CLOTHING RETURNS

THE TRAP OF "EASY RETURNS"

What does limiting clothing returns have to do with wardrobe care? Nothing directly. But it does have an impact on reducing wasteful spending and ultimately the impact of clothing dumping in landfills.

In today's shopping world, the easy return of unwanted clothing to retailers has become standard practice. Many stores employ liberal return policies as part of their strategy to improve sales. The idea is that it is easier for consumers to make the decision to buy merchandise when they know it is easy to return them.

The boom in online sales has substantially increased those return rates. The reason is simple. Not being able to see an item in person may prompt a buyer to order multiple sizes or colors to try on at home, and then ship or take back what they don't want; with shipping paid for by the retailer both ways in some cases.

According to a recent report, clothing and shoes bought online typically have the highest return rate. The average is 30 to 40 percent of items being returned. This is worse at holiday time, with post-holiday returns running into billions of dollars.

So what happens to clothing that has been returned to retailers? There are several scenarios:

- If the returned item is in unused or good condition, it will be returned to the sales floor.
- Some will be sent to be spruced up and repackaged.
- Others go to the discount channel, either to off-price retailers or wholesalers who specialize in reselling marked-down goods.
- Some returned goods are sold to companies who can

recycle the components or up-cycle the garment (re-fashion it into another garment).

These are the optimistic end results of returned clothing.

Many retailers end up throwing away over 25 percent of their returns. That means millions of pounds of goods end up in landfills a year as a result of returns.

Plus, keep in mind that shipping returns back to the retailer involves the cost of shipping material, fuel, processing and handling, and other expenses. This should be factored into what "free return shipping" actually costs. Although return-processing logistics and costs may be more pertinent to retailers than consumers, it is up to all of us to do our part to minimize our ecological footprint where we can.

*"My clothes are an extension of my personality.
I'd look awful in ladylike dresses."*

—*Carol Channing*

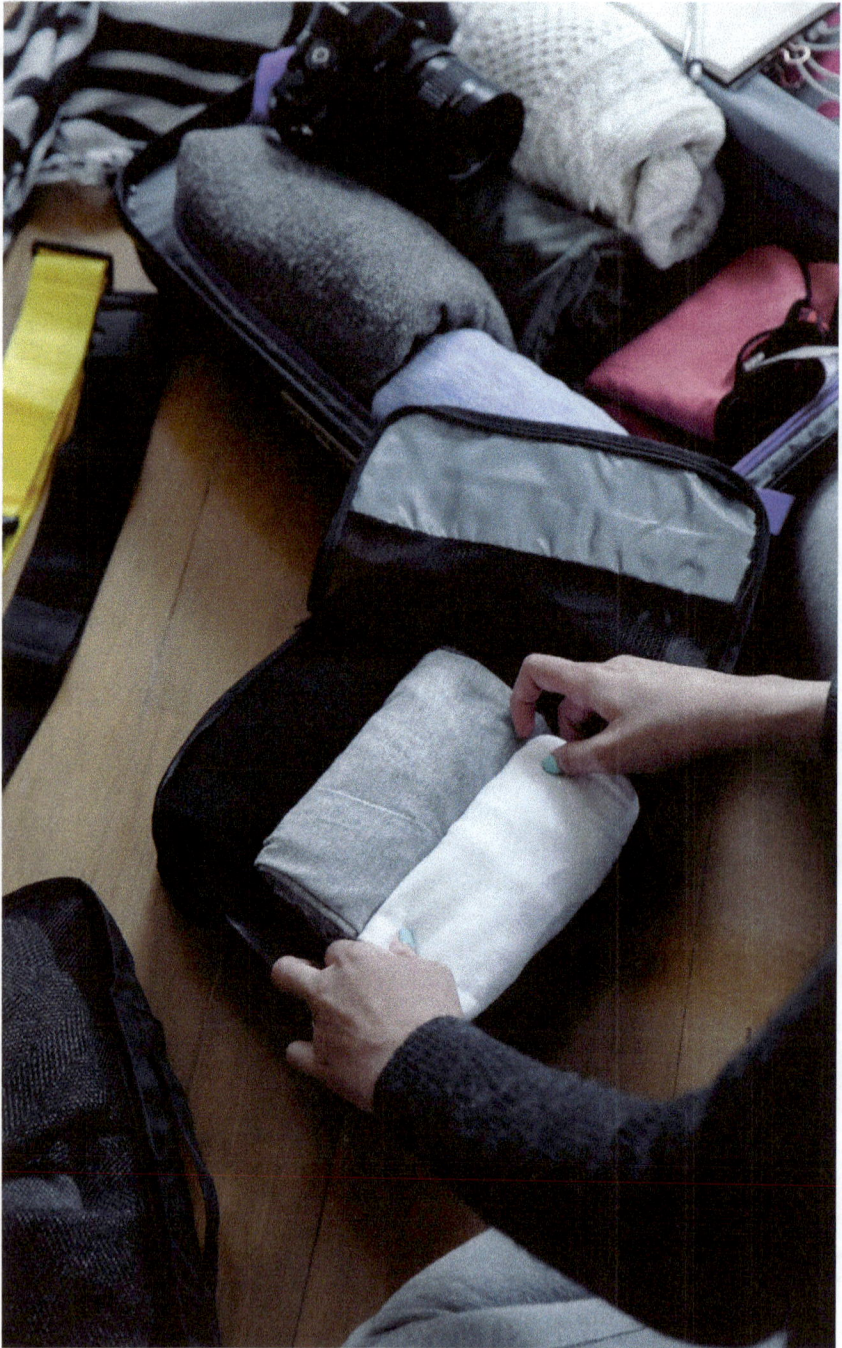

TRAVEL PACKING & CLOTHING DAMAGE

You may have had that "Oh no!" moment when you open your suitcase upon arrival at your destination and find unexpected wardrobe mishaps. The problem can be made worse if things are packed tightly together so that, for example, spilled cream has permeated garments throughout the suitcase.

What are some common causes of ruined clothing on trips?

- Increased cost of check-in bags has inspired many of us to try to fit as much as possible into our carry-on. This means items jammed into a suitcase can cause damage to fabrics, including snags and tears.

- Liquid containers (like lotions and makeup) can leak or explode at high altitudes. All containers have air in them, which will be at ground level pressure before take off. Once at high altitude, the air inside the container expands. So spillage might occur if the container is not tightly closed. Or worse yet, the container might burst.

- Improper packing of delicate silks or other fabrics can result in clothes being a wrinkled mess upon arrival.

- Transfer of dirt and odors can occur from packing worn and clean items tightly into the same luggage.

With some precaution and forethought about packing, much potential damage and resulting stress can be minimized even in today's challenging, restrictive travel environment.

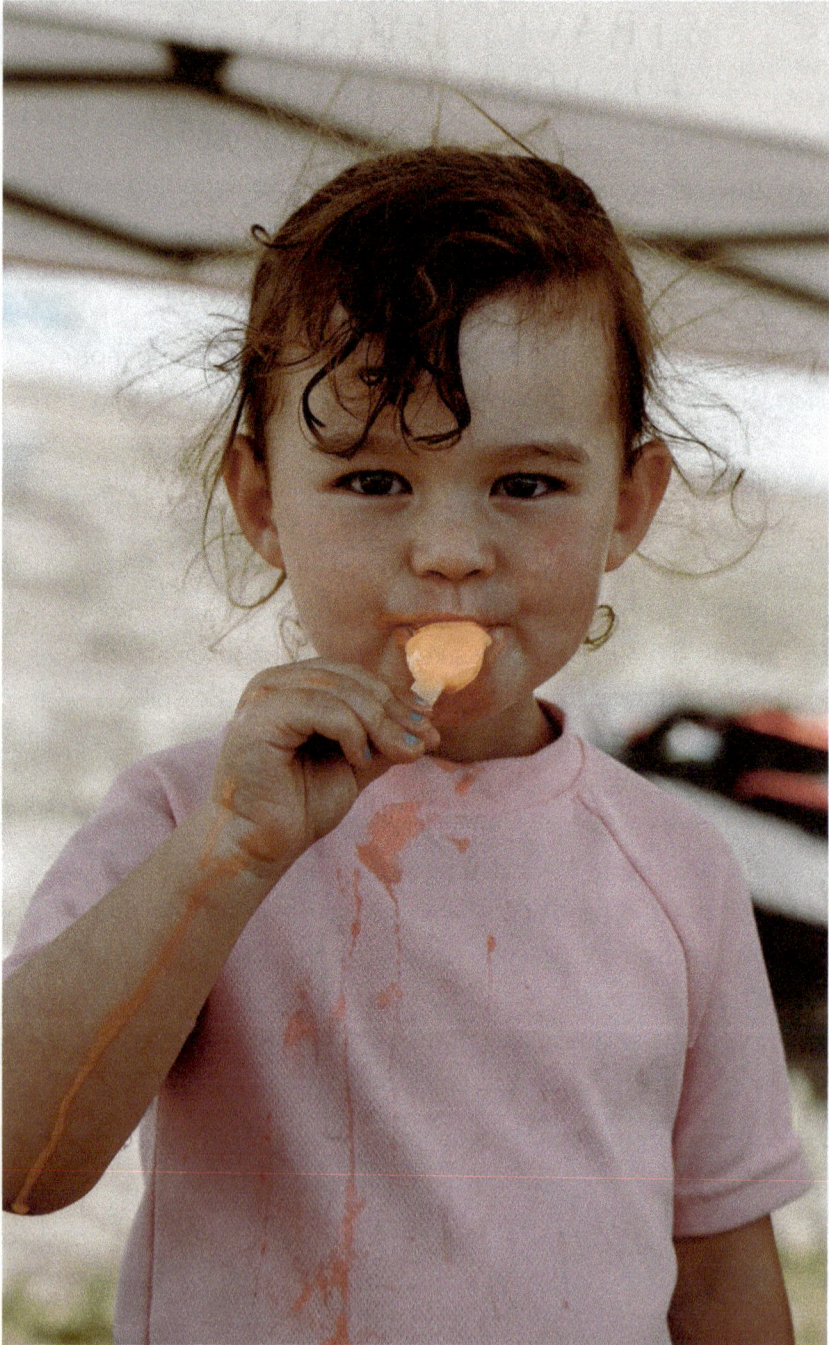

KIDS CLOTHING CONCERNS

For parents, dressing up their little ones is fun. Those outfits can be so cute! The other side, of course, is the concern about how much you invest in something that has such short duration.

One recent study shows that in the latter part of 2020 children's clothing exceeded $250 billion in global sales. This means that a massive amount of children's clothing will go through the process of being worn, recycled and possibly discarded.

Why does clothing for children have a shorter useful life than adult clothing?

GROWTH SPURTS

Children experience growth spurts that often out pace the clothing that is bought for them. On average, children grow out of their clothes every six months, for babies it is about 10 weeks. While donating or re-selling used clothing is an option, the sheer volume means that if items are not in pristine condition they may end up in landfills, just like adult clothing.

WARDROBE MESSES

Children and wardrobe messes seem to go hand-in-hand, as they explore the world and go through the usual childhood developmental phases. For babies, it includes spit ups and leaks. For toddlers and kids it shifts to accidental food spills from self-feeding; plus dirt and damage from active playing.

These factors can lead to the types of damage that consign them to being discarded to landfills.

ADAPTING TO FASHION TRENDS

There is an increase in kids clothing which mirrors the trends in grownup apparel. We see it in matching "parent and mini" styles that are a popular fashion trend. It appeals to the recent generation of parents who want a more sophisticated look for their kids—one that complements their own fashion sense.

Social media has also played an important part in this direction, with the influence of "celebrity kids" on constant view in our feeds, and stylish parents posting pictures of their little ones on popular sites.

The desire to copy trends is great for looking chic in the moment. But this can also give rise to the desire to discard clothing items once a trend is over, rather than seeing them as a viable "hand-me-down" to the next generation.

In the wake of the current ecological crisis of clothing dumping, there are some children's-wear design companies who have built their model around longevity, with quality fabrics and designs that can stand the test of time, and have a high likelihood of being passed down to siblings.

STAND-ALONE RETAIL STORES

In recent years, there has been a surge in designer brands and major labels opening stores that are dedicated to their kids-wear collection. This makes sense from a business perspective. They can control production and branding, and sell directly to consumers (cutting out the department store slice in their profits).

Along with store openings, of course, comes lots of promotional offers, continuous new collections (and perhaps tie-ins with influencer spokespeople). It pretty much mimics the fast fashion model.

With these dizzying options it is understandable that, like adult closets, little ones' closets are also filled to the brim with clothing—some barely worn or not worn at all before they are outgrown. Also like their adult counterparts, donating or discarding has become the perpetual necessity to keep kids' closets ready for the next batch of must-haves.

"Clothes and manners do not make the man; but, when he is made, they greatly improve his appearance."

—*Henry Ward Beecher*

PART 2 — A NEW APPROACH TO WARDROBE CARE

THE CIRCULAR FASHION ECONOMY

The Circular Fashion Economy

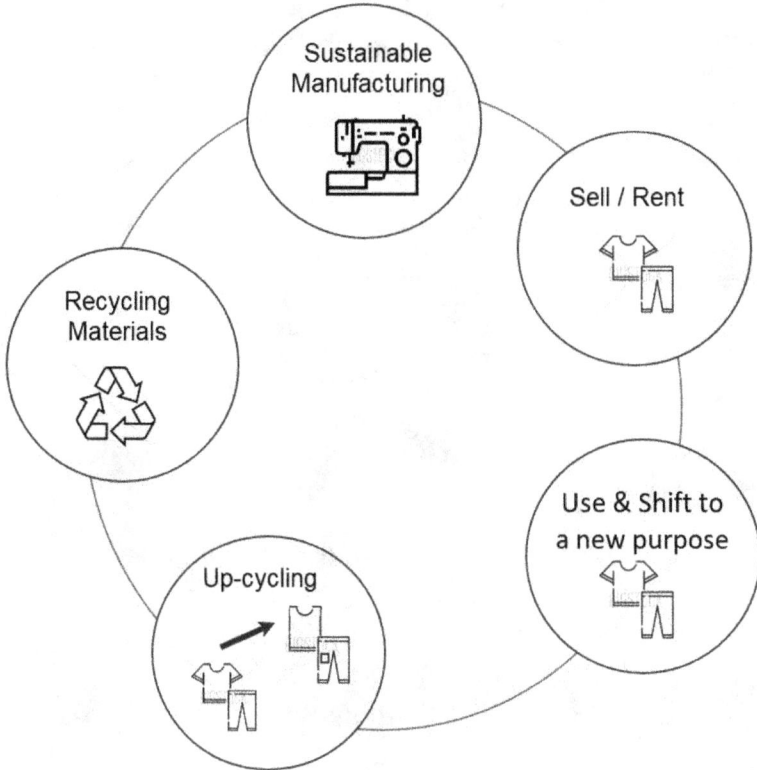

In recent years we have seen the rise in the "Circular Fashion Economy." This is one which clothing (and its components) are kept in a revolving cycle for as long as possible.

It is an approach that combines sustainable practices with regenerative end uses for all phases of the garment's life cycle. There are several stages in the Circular Fashion Economy.

SUSTAINABLE MANUFACTURING

Designers are joining in the effort to be more eco-conscious of their manufacturing processes.

There have been tremendous strides made in the innovation of garments made from non-traditional fibers. These include:

- Recycled plastic bottles
- New plant-based fibers (from bananas, bamboo, hemp, soy, etc.)
- Recycling discarded clothing.
- Certified organic fabrics made without the use of harmful pesticides.
- Dead stock fabrics (Left over materials from seasons past) used to create new collections.

Manufacturing process may also extend to:

- Sourcing trims that are made form recycled material
- Using recycled packaging for shipment
- Using alternative energy sources (such as solar) to power factory machines and lighting.

SELL/RENT

Selling new clothing to customers remains the main priority of retail fashion businesses. It sustains vital parts of the fashion industry (fabric mills, trim companies, sewing factories, etc.); and accounts for the majority of the multi-trillion dollars spent on clothing and accessories each year.

That being said, there has been a boom in the clothing rental market within the past few years, with annual sales in the multi-billion dollars. The trend has extended beyond renting formal dresses and into everyday wear. The reasons are simple.

- It is more eco-friendly than buying clothing that may end up being discarded.
- It gives consumers a way to try new fashion trends without making a commitment that may hang in their closet for years to come.
- It is an economical way to keep closets fresh with new fashions.

Major luxury brands and designers are following the lead of companies who are successfully renting everything from clothing to accessories. This gives them entry into the rental market, additional sales opportunities, control over the final disposition of their merchandise and support of the ethical values of the brand.

USE & SHIFT CLOTHING TO OTHER PURPOSES

You might be surprised to hear from your favorite department store that they now offer "gently used" outfits, at great savings.

One of retail's biggest new trends isn't just about offering what is new. It is about reselling previously-worn merchandise. And it is booming! Recent reports have shown that the resale clothing market is growing much faster than traditional retail, and is estimated to be worth more than double that of fast fashion, at over $80 billion, within the next decade.

Why the growth in this retail trend? It is appealing to a conscious consumer who is growing increasingly concerned about disposable fast-fashion. It is also a more economical way to invest in new clothing. It's no surprise, then, that retail giants on all ends of the market have been strengthening their position in resale.

Some are creating "buy back" programs, where customers can return used brand clothing in exchange for credits to put toward a new purchase. This keeps loyal customers coming back while at the same time appealing to a new base that is concerned about the ecological impact of throwing away old clothing.

Some retailers have even launched websites dedicated to the resale of their merchandise, donating some of the proceeds to organizations supporting ecological care. It is a win/win for all concerned.

It is the perfect combination of Buy Good/Feel Good.

UP-CYCLING CLOTHES

The song "Everything Old is New Again" gets a new twist with this trend.

Up-cycling clothes that already exist is one way to ensure sustainability, because it promotes the idea of circular fashion. To "up-cycle" is to take something already made and turn it into a fresh item rather than seeking out new raw materials to start from scratch. It is a creative way for designers to re-imagine older clothes and keep them in circulation rather than having them head to the landfill.

Some designer labels are proudly announcing special edition garments or accessories made from returns or end-of-bolt fabric remnants. In some cases, the new items come at a premium price due to the labor involved in disassembling the existing garments and creatively coordinating the material to create something new.

Loyal customers to these brands are embracing the price. Responding both to the idea of getting a one-of-a-kind design and the company's effort to reduce ecological waste.

There are different ways to up-cycle clothing. These include:
• Deconstructing existing garments to create new patchwork garments with the parts.
• Adding embellishments to an existing garment.
• Turning clothing into bags and other accessories.

RECYCLING MATERIALS

So, what happens when garments have reached the end of their wearable cycle? There is a growing market to capture them before they end up in landfills and turn them back into fibers to create new fabrics and other end uses.

THE RECYCLING PROCESS

For fabrics to be recycled, there are fundamental differences between natural and synthetic fibers.

For natural textiles, the incoming garments are sorted by type of material and color. They are then pulled into fibers or shredded, sometimes introducing other fibers into the yarn. The yarn is then cleaned and spun. It is now ready for use in weaving or knitting.

For polyester-based textiles, garments are shredded and then granulated for processing into polyester chips. These are subsequently melted and used to create new fibers for use in new polyester fabrics.

"How can anyone be silly enough to think himself better than other people, because his clothes are made of finer woolen thread than theirs. After all, those fine clothes were once worn by a sheep, and they never turned it into anything better than a sheep."

—*Thomas More*

PART 3 – THE SOLUTIONS

SOLUTIONS

DEFINING WARDROBE CARE

WHAT DO WE MEAN BY WARDROBE?

We mean anything that you wear or carry to help you maintain your appearance and personal well being. This includes:

- clothing
- accessories (belts, hats)
- shoes
- purses
- jewelry
- personal care items (makeup, cleansers, hygiene aids, etc.)

WHAT DO WE MEAN BY CARE?

Wardrobe care covers the entirety of your wardrobe's life cycle. It begins with consideration about purchases and ends with how best to transition items out. In between these two concerns, it is about how to best protect, store and organize your wardrobe. This includes best-practices for avoiding:

- pest damage (from moths and silver fish)
- fading
- stretching garments out of shape from improper storage
- shrinkage
- mold
- stains from accidental spills
- fiber deterioration

There are many things to consider when it comes to proper wardrobe care. The type of wardrobe item, the fabrication, intended use and cleaning requirements are just some of the factors involved. The intent of this guide is to give you an overview for care and maintenance. Plus, handy worksheets and checklists are included to make the task a bit easier.

BE CONSCIENTIOUS ABOUT WARDROBE PURCHASES

BE THOUGHTFUL ABOUT FABRICS IN GARMENTS YOU BUY

The textile industry has come under scrutiny for the amount of resources needed for manufacturing certain fabrics. For example, studies have shown that it takes more than 20,000 liters (5,283 gallons) of water to produce just one kilogram (2.2 pounds) of cotton, which roughly equals one tee shirt and a pair of jeans.

On the other hand, cotton is a plant-based, renewable resource that supports an important global economy. There are several organizations working to support farmer-level improvement to reduce water use, and to implement other efforts to make cotton farming more sustainable.

We also see innovations in fabric manufacturing (e.g. using recycled fibers and plastic bottles) to improve production and reduce negative ecological impact.

CONSIDER THE SUSTAINABILITY OF GARMENTS EMBELLISHED WITH SEQUINS AND GLITTER

Glitter and sequins look great for party dresses and other formal wear. However, they pose a new threat to the environment.

Glitter and sequins are usually made from PVC plastic or aluminum. Laundering garments with these embellishments can cause tiny pieces to pass through the filtration systems in sewage facilities and end up in our waterways and oceans.

These PVC plastics are also not biodegradable. They can sit in our water supply for hundreds of years. When it comes to underwater ecosystems, the effects are harmful.

When small materials like sequins and glitter enter the oceans, they are ingested by small organisms. These organisms might be more attracted to the sparkle of the glitter. They ingest them, and pass them along to the fish who feed on them and other animals up the food chain.

A recent study has shown that the negative impacts caused by marine ingestion of these materials may also have detrimental effects on humans. We are potentially consuming marine life, which contain micro plastic from sequins and glitter. Micro plastics, when ingested, can produce toxic, bio-accumulative chemicals including carcinogens and hormone disruptors.

There is some good news. There are companies working on biodegradable sequins made from cellulose (a natural plant fiber) and recycled material. Some brands have switched to embroideries and embellishments that have the richness of details we love, without the damaging effects on the waterways and wildlife.

BUY MORE SUSTAINABLY-PRODUCED PRODUCTS

A good option that can be done on a small level? Focus on spending, when possible, on goods made from sustainably-produced materials and manufacturing methods (e.g. made from recycled materials, water-saving techniques, etc.)

This is a small investment that will make a big impact in the environment and support the textile industry, which is looking for ways to respond to consumer demands.

THINK ABOUT THE ADVANTAGES OF WASHABLE GARMENTS VS. DRY CLEANING

How much of your wardrobe is washable? How much is "dry clean only"? The proportion of each in your closet is a personal one, of course, based on the types of garments you love. It might be prudent to evaluate that percentage, to make sure that the balance between the two meets your budget and eco-concerns.

There are definitely pros and cons to both forms of cleaning your garments. Here are a few things to consider on both sides.

Washable Garments
Pros

- It is easy to put something in the wash versus having to make a special trip to have it cleaned.
- It is less expensive than dry cleaning.
- Certain fabrics that may seem "dry clean only" are actually washable. Be sure to check the label for care instruction.

Cons

- There might be a tendency to over-launder garments or use improper techniques (too-hot water, or level of wash cycle). These can lead to faster fiber deterioration.
- Washing detergents can also cause skin irritation (like dry cleaning chemicals). There are companies now offering "green" alternatives (detergent sheets and non-plastic packaging).

Dry Clean Only Garments
Pros

- Garments that are embellished or require special cleaning will be safer with proper dry cleaning.
- Dry cleaning can save the time and effort of mundane tasks like starching and pressing cotton attire.
- Cumbersome or large items may not be possible to wash at home.
- There are now "at home" dry cleaning kits that offer an

option to save time and money.

- There are products now offered that are a safer, more eco-friendly alternative to traditional dry cleaning chemicals.

Cons

- Perchloroethylene (PERC) is the most common solvent used for dry cleaning in the United States. According to a recent EPA finding, it presents an unreasonable risk of injury to human health, under certain uses. This is not to say that the chemical is guaranteed to cause injury, but that it has this capability.
- PERC is designated a Hazardous Air Pollutant (HAP) under the Clean Air Act (CAA), a hazardous waste under the Comprehensive Environmental Response, Compensation and Liability Act (CERCLA) and a regulated drinking water contaminant under the Safe Drinking Water Act (SDWA).
- Health reactions to dry cleaning chemicals can range from mild (skin rash) to more severe respiratory ones.

ADAPT A "COST-PER-WEAR" MINDSET

The Cost Per Wear (CPW) lets you understand the real price of your clothes. It can also help you think about purchases to decide if it is cost-effective.

The Cost Per Wear (CPW) is a formula that averages out cost of the garment divided by the number of times you wear it. The more you wear something, the lower its Cost Per Wear. If you wear something only once, its CPW is the full purchase price of the item. If you wear that item multiple times, the Cost Per Wear is lower.

For example, if you have a blouse that you bought for $50 and you wore it 50 times, the CPW of that blouse is $1 ($50 ÷ 50 times worn = $1). So instead of a one-time $50 purchase, you should think of it as paying $1 every time you wear that blouse.

The goal is to get your wardrobe to the point where you have a better CPW for the majority of the items in your closet. Be realistic in calculating the likelihood of wearing an item multiple times. Ask yourself, "How often will I really wear this?" If you think it will be a lot, consider if you have similar items in your closet. For example, many of us may own a sizable collection of tee shirts. How often will it really be in rotation? This can help you to decide if it is worth the investment.

RE-IMAGINE THE VALUE OF WARDROBE PURCHASES

It begins by asking the question, "What are the end goals of purchasing wardrobe items?" Are they to be part of your go-to basics for as long as possible? Used for a season or two then resold or donated? Stored as a keepsake? Reserved for special events or occasions?

Having the end-goal in mind makes it easier to be motivated to give proper care for these purchases. Whether the goal is to increase the longevity of wear, improve the resale value, or protect against damages (pest, fading, mold and more) that can result in items being discarded to landfills. Here are some recommended rules of thumb:

TREAT ALL WARDROBE INVESTMENTS AS IMPORTANT

Treating all wardrobe investments as equal helps to eliminate a "throw away" mentality towards the things we buy, thus fostering a more eco-friendly mind set.

We often place a higher wardrobe care priority on more expensive items. We may think, "Oh it's just a $10 top from the bargain store." The perception is that there is reduced value in it, than say a $200 top from a high-end brand. This hierarchy of perceived value makes it easier to throw that $10 top into the garbage than to put effort into its care for a renewed after-life.

Price and quality alone does not guarantee longevity of wear. What is important is giving all of your wardrobe proper care, no matter the price point. The maxim "buying quality over quantity" is a wise way to think. A wardrobe item of higher quality fabrics and construction will wear longer. That being said, will a moth eat a hole as easily in a $20 sweater as in a $400 one, if not properly cared for? The answer is YES! The quality of care is as important as the cost of the garment.

CONSIDER WHAT PERCENTAGE OF YOUR BUDGET YOU SPEND ON A PARTICULAR WARDROBE ITEM.

This will raise the perception of its value, worthiness of purchase, and the importance of its care.

It is all about investment percentage. A $20 top is 20% of a discretionary budget of $100. A $100 top is 20% of a discretionary budget of $500. So, that $20 top is the same investment percentage as the $100 top. And thus has the same relative value. It deserves to be treated with the same respect.

CONSIDER THE ECOLOGICAL IMPACT OF WARDROBE DISPOSAL

As we know:
- The volume of clothing thrown away each year has doubled in the last 20 years, from 7 million to well over 11 million tons.
- Textiles can take up to 200+ years to decompose in landfills.

- 84 percent of of disposed clothing ends up in landfills or in-cinerators. Not (as we'd like to think) recycled into other use-ful purposes.

The good news is that, just like recycling our cans and bottles, small measures taken by each of us can have significant impact!

BUY LESS

It goes without saying that buying less is a good rule of thumb. It's like a diet, though. The temptations are always there and we are accustomed to wanting what is new and fresh. The "one thing in — one thing out" philosophy is a good way to manage clutter and keep a minimalist mindset in spending. This way, you are investing in items for long-term use and curtailing the mindset of discarding unwanted impulse buys.

BE CONSISTENT IN CARING FOR YOUR WARDROBE

Like timely car maintenance, taking proactive measures to keep your wardrobe in good shape will help to make things last longer and minimize the need for untimely disposal. This includes proper laundering, storage and overall maintenance.

THINK RECYCLE AND RE-USE

Probably the most important thing you can do is to consider alternatives to throwing away your unwanted or damaged wardrobe items. Donating, repairing, re-selling or re-purposing these items are great options. There are many resources available to help in this matter. See our resource chapter for some ideas.

That being said, remember that as far as items being donated or re-sold — no-one wants junk! Think of these items as a gift you are handing down, not trash being thrown out. You want them to be in relatively good shape and attractive to the recipient (this goes back to caring for your wardrobe to maintain the highest quality possible). Do a quick inspection before parting with items to see if you would purchase them at the local thrift store, and always ask the question before investing your money in new things: "What are the end goals of wardrobe items being purchased?"

"If you love something, wear it all the time... Find things that suit you. That's how you look extraordinary."

— Vivienne Westwood

PEST CONTROL

The key to minimizing pest damage to clothing is to keep in mind that pests are (A) attracted to the fabric itself (the keratin in animal fibers like wool and silk) or (B) Attracted to the detritus left in clothing such as food, drinks, perspiration, and dead skin.

- Consistently clean items before storing.
- Air out worn items and do a quick brush to remove particles before putting them away.
- Scents such as lavender, moth balls and cedar act as a deterrent. If however the female insect has laid eggs in the garment, it will not kill the larvae that hatch. Cleaning garments before storage is the best defense.
- Vacuum and dust closets periodically and check for evidence of pest infestation (abandoned casings, dropping, etc.)
- Use proper containers for long term storage. There are many different thoughts on what that means.
  - Plastic containers — If using plastic, the general rule is to use one that is airtight to keep out bugs. But be aware that plastic containers may not allow air to circulate. This can lead to mustiness and mildew.
  - Cotton containers — These protect against pests while allowing air to circulate. The same rules apply as with plastic containers. Be sure to clean the garments before storage and place the containers in an area that is not hot and humid.

THE ECO-SMART APPROACH TO BUYING CLOTHES ONLINE

So, how can you improve the chances that clothing you buy online is of good quality, has a complementary fit, and will most likely stay in rotation in your closet? Plus, minimize the cost and effort associated with doing returns? Here are some ideas.

TRUST FAMILIAR BRAND NAMES FOR THE MAJOR PURCHASES

It is great to branch out with something new. That being said, a tried and trusted brand has a higher guarantee of delivering what you expect in terms of quality and fit.

PAY ATTENTION TO FABRIC CONTENT

Companies spend a great deal of effort to create beautiful images for their online store. It can be disappointing if the product, upon delivery, does not match what you saw online. Checking the fabric content will give you a good idea of how the garment may look in person. For example, if you own 100% cotton garments then you will have a pretty good idea of how a similar garment purchased online will appear when you receive it.

LOOK AT COMPANY HISTORY AND REVIEWS

Positive or negative reviews by proven, paid customers are a wonderful way to know if garments might work for you. Look for feedback about general things like the fit, fabric and durability.

Sometimes the company history, founder's reason for starting the company or general philosophy can give you a clue as to how their products will perform.

For example, if a company selling surfing gear is started by a surfer you can imagine that he/she has designed products based on their own personal needs. Their products are more likely to solve the same personal needs that you may have if you surf. They will also most likely be obsessed with quality and performance. If they belong to a community of surfers who love their products, it can be a good bet that it might work for you. Loyal users usually signal strong performance with clothing and accessory products.

How long has the company been in business? Longevity might be something to consider, if making a pricey purchase. Remember, companies pour a lot of marketing dollars into their online presence. Being in business over 10 years, for example, shows that they have staying power and have built loyalty by providing customers with quality products.

RETHINK YOUR BUDGET SPLIT BETWEEN ONLINE AND IN-STORE PURCHASES

While it might be tempting to do almost all of your clothing purchases online, nothing beats the hands-on experience of seeing and trying on garments in person. It might be good to consider splitting your budget (for example 60% online/40% in person) to improve the likelihood of keeping something fabulous that you have tried on.

LIMIT IMPULSE BUYING

An impulse buy is anytime you purchase something you weren't planning to. If it's not planned for in your budget ahead of time, it's an impulse buy. Even if it is something tempting in the checkout that seems very inexpensive.

When it comes to clothing, impulse buying because of sale promotions and easy returns are enticing invitations. The issue is that unwanted and unworn clothing can either sit in our closets and become clutter or become part of the aforementioned hidden cost of returns (shipping materials, processing and dumping in landfills if the return is soiled and unwearable).

CONSIDER PUTTING CLOTHING BUDGET ON A GIFT CARD

The old school idea of shopping with cash doesn't work online, of course. It is easy to go over budget and have buyer's remorse when you check your account balance.

If your allotted fashion budget is on a card that is independent from your checking account, you may be more careful about buying decisions, as you check available balance on that card. Be realistic in setting goals. Seasonal purchases may require a slightly higher budget than ongoing need.

TRAVEL AND WARDROBE CARE

There is a lot to consider when packing for a trip. This includes the climate, accommodations, length of stay, and special wardrobe requirements. Packing as light as possible is a good rule of thumb, but as important is making sure that your wardrobe arrives in good condition.

PICK CLOTHING IN STURDY, EASY CARE FABRICS

When you are away from home, you want to make sure that your wardrobe can stand up to the rigors of travel. Here are a few things to consider:

- Leave "dry clean only" garments at home. Instead, opt for items in fabrics that can be easily washed in a hotel room to remove minor stains.
- If you need to carry clothing with delicate beading, lace and other embellishments, be sure to protect them in your suitcase. Wrapping them with tissue or other articles of clothing is a great option.

SEPARATE BY CATEGORY

Usually, when it comes to categories we think in terms of tops, bottoms, shoes etc. It is also important to keep in mind the potential damage that the items can cause. The main subcategories are:

- Liquids - Be sure to keep liquid products (like lotions and foundation) in a separate area from your clothing. The last thing you want is for a leak or exploding bottle to ruin your outfits. Remember also that zip-closure plastic bags are not guaranteed to be leak-proof. So, double bag liquid items to be safe.

- Worn items – This refers primarily to shoes. Remember that whatever shoes you are packing has been through dirt and other elements. Be sure to pack them in a separate bag before integrating them into your luggage. This also applies to items that are not freshly laundered. Keep them separate to avoid the possible transfer of dirt, perfumes, and other odors to new items.

FOR CLOTHING, THINK FLAT AND VERSATILE

Wrinkle-resistant fabrics like rayon, silk or microfiber take up less space than denim, cotton or fleece and are less likely to be a wrinkled mess upon your arrival.

BE PREPARED FOR FASHION EMERGENCIES

As far as taking care of any wardrobe emergencies, be sure to pack a repair kit. You can purchase a pre-made one or create a DIY kit from things you have at home. Here is a list of some must-haves that covers basic mishaps.

- Travel sewing kit*
- Stain removal wipes or pen

- Fashion tape
- A few buttons
- Alcohol wipes
- Underarm deodorant shields

An alternative to a full blown sewing kit is to thread a needle with a long strand of neutral color. Secure the needle through a piece of paper and wind the thread around the needle. Fold paper over to cover needle tip. Do the same to a few safety pins and you're set.

WARDROBE CARE FOR KIDS

While it can be challenging to keep little ones looking spotless throughout the day, there are some basic things that can be done to increase the likelihood that their clothing will last as long as possible, and be passed down to siblings or to be successfully resold, if that is the desire. Here are a few ideas.

BUY FABRICS THAT CAN WITHSTAND MULTIPLE WASHINGS

It goes without saying that most kids clothing will go through the wash cycle many times. Investing in clothing made of sturdy fabrics that are easy to clean will improve the chances of them surviving long enough to be passed on to another child after use.

BUY GARMENTS WITHOUT SEQUINS AND INTRICATE EMBELLISHMENTS

How you would launder your dressy dress with sequins? Would you throw it in the washing machine? Probably not. This is pretty much what is done with kid tops with sparkly sequin mermaids, unicorns and action figures. They look great on the hanger but may not hold up under lots of play and multiple spins in the washing machine.

The other potential problem is that sequins are made of PVC plastics that do not biodegrade. So, if garment are thrown away, they can sit in landfills for hundreds of years. If sequins or other sparkles enter the ocean, they can harm wildlife who eat them (attracted by the shimmer and thinking they are food) and other animals up the food chain.

Garments with high-end trims like lace, tassels and sewn-on flowers should be fine. As long as they are handled with care during the wash cycle.

LOOK FOR HIGHER QUALITY GARMENTS FOR BASICS

It is tempting to buy lower-priced clothing on the premise that "kids will outgrow them soon anyway." But it is important to think in terms of passing it down to the next generation.

Higher quality garments, especially basics that are worn frequently, stand a greater chance of making it through their stage of growth. Having a balanced mix of higher end and lower priced items is a good goal for kids wear.

Look for features like reinforced knees, buttons that are securely sewn and clean finished seams.

PREP FOR WARDROBE EMERGENCIES

Just as with adult clothing, catching stains before they set is critical to longevity of wear. We recommend carrying stain wipes or pen in your bag. If kids get a stain or spill on their clothing, a quick dab with one of these treatment solutions may help keep stains from becoming permanent before you get a chance to wash them.

"Sweater, n. Garment worn by child when its mother is feeling chilly."

— Ambrose Bierce

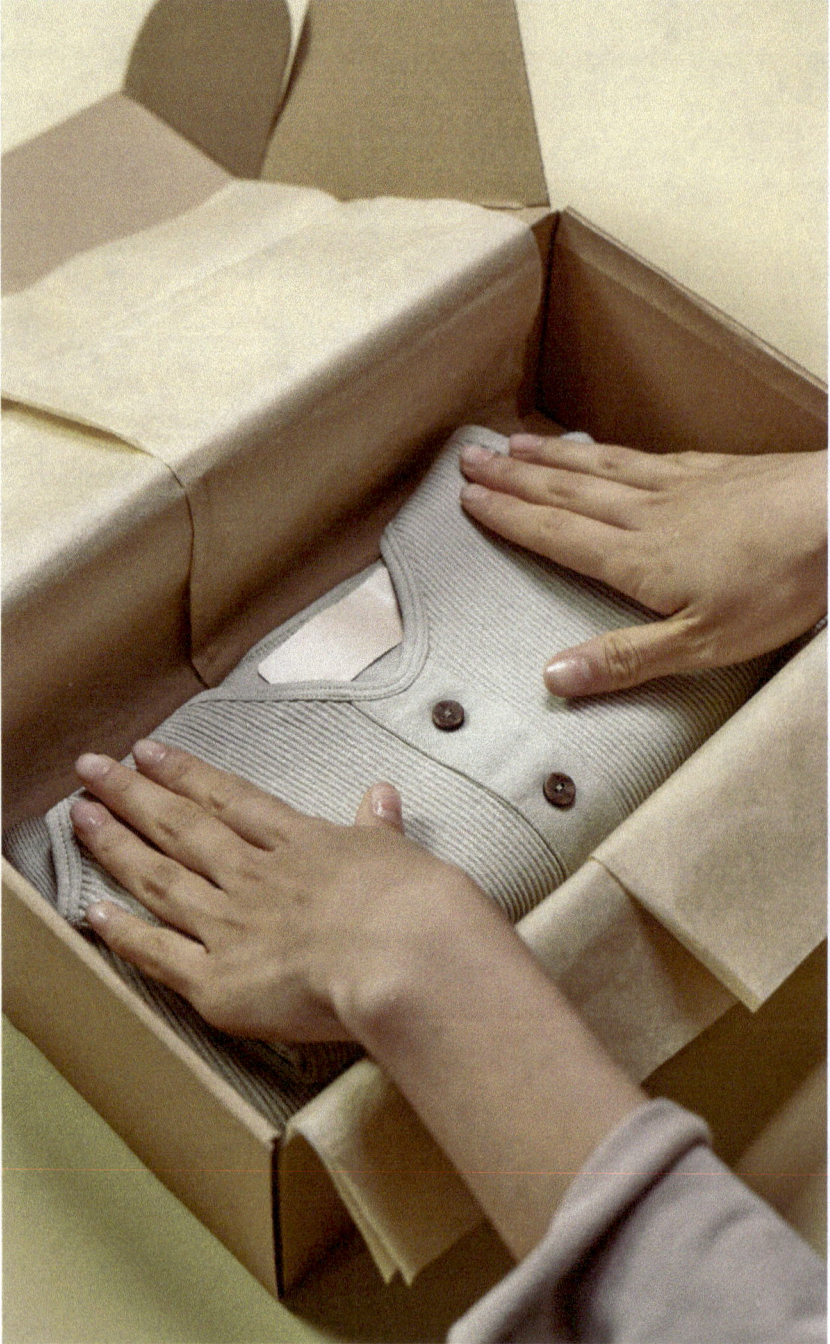

BE THOUGHTFUL ABOUT CLOTHING RETURNS

While returns are inevitable, making sure we invest in clothing that will stick around in our closets and be regularly worn is one way to reduce wasteful spending and returns that could end up in landfills. Here are a few things to consider.

A SAFE WAY TO TRY NEW COLORS.

That bright orange dress looks amazing on the model in the magazine and the color is the hottest trend. The temptation to go outside our comfort zone with colors is tempting (and can be a good thing). If unsure of the color, consider doing it with an accent item (like a tee shirt or jewelry) that can easily be incorporated into your regular wardrobe.

STICK TO THE TRIED AND TRUE FOR BASICS.

Found a favorite brand of jeans, pants or jacket? Great! If you like the cut and the way it makes you feel, then let these be your "go-to" for replacement. You can experiment with new colors in the tried-and-true cut. This keeps you on trend and also reduces the likelihood of returning the item.

BUY TO SUIT YOUR PERSONAL STYLE

Much has been written about finding your signature style. This can and will change with time and circumstances (new job, family life, health needs, age, etc). However, throughout the twists and turns of lifestyle changes, there are always certain patterns that will remain constant.

For example, do you grab jeans and tee shirt for most of your basic wardrobe needs? Do you gravitate to leggings and a slouchy top? What stores do you shop for inspiration? These overall patterns are a clue to where you should focus your wardrobe investments. You are more likely to keep items if they fit your core style.

The average wardrobe usage breaks down like this:

- About 15% is worn on a regular basis (and probably truly reflects your personal style)
- Then there is around 25% that you wear sometimes, but not that often. They are okay but maybe not your top "go-to.
- About 20% are specialty wear (cocktail attire, sentimental outfits that you love).
- The remaining 40% are clothing that you don't like and you know it, but you aren't ready to say goodbye to just yet.

The goal should be to push that 15% of items worn on a regular basis to 30% or more. This is truly when you will have a lean closet that reflects your personal style and reduces impulse buying and returns.

TRYING ON GARMENTS FROM ONLINE PURCHASE

You've got that wonderful outfit you saw and bought online. Great! Now it is time to see how it looks.

Think of it like a gift that you have received and might want to re-gift to the next person if it doesn't work for you. Care should be taken in how the garment is handled and repackaged for return. Here are a few ideas.

- Leave the tags on the garment and liners in swimsuit or other intimate apparel.
- Remove jewelry that might snag the fabric if it is delicate (like lace or loosely woven knit).
- Make sure you are not wearing makeup that might smudge into the garment. Use a face guard to protect necklines, if necessary.
- Consider wearing a bodysuit or body shaper. It will give a better overall fit and keep the garment free from lotions and perspiration stains.
- Don't try on a garment if wearing perfumes that might transfer during try-on.
- If you have used skin lotion, hair products and other liquid emulsions, make sure they are dry before try-on.
- If the garment does not suit your needs or liking, refold neatly into the packaging and return box.

USE THE WARDROBE RESALE MARKET

Thinking about cleaning out your closet but looking for the best ways to lighten your clothing load? There are many ways to go about it. It depends on your needs and time availability. Here are a few ideas.

ONLINE SELLING

The online resell market is a booming business, with many options to list your clothing in order to recoup your investment. This includes major social media platforms and online businesses dedicated to re-selling clothing and accessories.

The thing to remember is that items should be presented in the best condition possible.

- Make sure items are cleaned.
- Take photographs (if posting online) that show the item to its best advantage.
- Use descriptors that catch the eye. Think about what would get your attention (fabric content, versatility of use, etc.)

- Be honest about the condition of the items (misleading information can have a negative impact on your rating, if you plan to use the platform for future reselling).
- Batch items together, if possible, to get the best opportunity to clear items more quickly out of your closet.
- If the site offers the option for "Free Shipping," consider adding that. You can buffer the price you offer with a little bit more to offset shipping cost.

GARAGE OR ESTATE SALES

If selling clothing items is your goal, holding garage or estate sales are good options. People love to find bargains at these types of events. Things like high-value home accessories, sports gear and vintage products are typically the most sought-after items. Clothing (unless it is a rare piece) is more common, so may not be as desirable. Some of the same rules apply as with selling online.

- Batch items together, if possible, to get the best opportunity to clear items more quickly out of your closet.
- It is unlikely that you will wash and press items, but try to make them presentable (hung on a rack, folded, labeled, sorted in bags, etc.) to give the best presentation possible.

CONSIDER GIFTING AS A WAY TO PART WITH CLOTHING ITEMS

Perhaps there is someone in your circle of family and friends who would love that clothing item. They can be the first people to approach. The same rule applies to prepping that item, as with reselling it online. Be sure it is cleaned and perhaps even boxed as a gift. This will truly be regarded as something special rather than an unwanted cast off.

THINK OUTSIDE THE TRADITIONAL BOX TO DONATE ITEMS

As we have stated, donated garments, in poor condition, can end up being discarded to landfills or shipped to developing nations. These are some alternatives that are worth considering, since these clothing items go to fulfill important needs.

- Theatrical companies (for stage production costumes).
- Charities that provide clothing to people rebuilding their lives (with professional attire, etc.).
- Foster care programs (this is great for kids clothing).
- Refugee organizations that provide clothing and amenities to people fleeing their home countries.
- Emergency shelters for at-risk adults and children.

ONE ITEM IN, ONE ITEM OUT

This philosophy of removing an old item when we purchase a new one is a classic approach to keeping our closets streamlined.

It gives you the opportunity to really weigh purchasing decisions, if it means giving up something that may be of great value. The overall goal is to continually streamline your closet, so that the majority of items in it are worn often.

This starts from being mindful of purchases so that returns are limited. And continues with finding creative ways to pass along un-wanted items that will benefit both you and the environment.

STORE YOUR SHIPPING BOXES

Rather than recycling all those cardboard boxes in which you re-ceived your merchandise, keep a few in order to do returns. Simply cover or mark out the current retail labels. Some retailers will even provide returnable bags, which is a great way to promote responsible packaging re-use.

"Fashion is never in crisis because clothes are always necessary. "

—*Achille Maramotti*

TYPES OF WARDROBE CARE

Wardrobe maintenance runs the gamut from taking a few moments for quick care to more extensive cleaning a few times a year. We have broken down key types here, and also in easy reference forms at the back of the book.

- Everyday maintenance
- Spring maintenance
- Summer maintenance
- Fall maintenance
- Winter maintenance

PREPARATION

- First you will need a timer to make sure you don't go over.
- Next, do a one-time gathering of Wardrobe Care Tools you may need (see our suggested list in the guide).
- Pick your best solution.

EVERYDAY MAINTENANCE

Our days are generally filled with lots of activities (work, errands, home care and maybe child care). Thinking about wardrobe care may not be a priority, beyond doing laundry, or dealing with some pesky spill or wardrobe mishap that threatens to throw us off schedule.

What is important is developing quick, easy things that take no more than a few minutes but that can make a great difference in wardrobe up-keep. How much time do you have to devote daily to wardrobe care? We believe in keeping care time short and sweet. It's proactive and will create the satisfaction of knowing that you are on track with one thing on your list of a gazillion things to do! Got just a few minutes to do a quick wardrobe maintenance? Here's what you can do within these time frames. You will be surprised at how much you can get done.

2-MINUTE WARDROBE CARE

- Organize a few things (put on hanger, straighten, fold in drawer, etc.).
- De-clutter by putting one item in the donate/resell/repair basket.
- Run a brush over a few hanging tops and bottoms to pick up any food particles or other detritus that may be stuck in fibers (and that can attract pests).

5-MINUTE WARDROBE CARE

- Organize a few things (put on hanger, straighten, fold in drawer, etc.).
- De-clutter by putting one item in the donate/resell/repair basket.
- Run a brush over a few hanging tops and bottoms to pick up any food particles or other detritus that may be stuck in fibers (and that can attract pests).
- Do a quick wipe or buff a pair of shoes, purse, belt buckle).

10-MINUTE WARDROBE CARE

- Organize a few things (put on hanger, straighten, fold in drawer, etc.).
- De-clutter by putting one item in the donate/resell/repair basket
- Run a brush over a few hanging tops and bottoms to pick up any food particles or other detritus that may be stuck in fibers (and that can attract pests).
- Do a quick wipe or buff a pair of shoes, purse, belt buckle)
- Put away some laundry

SPRING WARDROBE MAINTENANCE

This is the time to put away winter gear and bring out the lighter wear. It is time for breezy cottons, sheer voile and linen to have their moment in the sun.

It seems easier to get your wardrobe ready for the spring season, right? The thinner, washable fabrics require less to maintain than woolens and leathers which may require specialty cleaning. Basically, it is toss in the wash and go! Even so, the same care and diligence should be applied to daily maintenance checks as with colder weather wear. Here are some things to keep in mind.

- Light color fabrics tend to show stains more than darker color fabrics. So, constant maintenance checks will ensure that you catch potentially fabric-damaging stains more quickly.
- Have a checklist as you go through each garment type to ensure that you are covering the basics.
- Remember that clothing moths are attracted to animal fibers. So, that lovely silk blouse or jacket may be a potential feast for those little pests. Be sure to protect silk clothing with pest repellents, as you do with woolens and mohair.
- Have the tools handy to take care of minor maintenance. More complex repairs can be set aside, so as not to slow down the process of daily maintenance.

SPRING WARDROBE MAINTENANCE CHECKLIST

Give a quick check for the following clothing items.

BLOUSES

- Stains
- Fraying or discoloration on collar
- Snags
- Holes from pests
- Loose buttons
- Embellishments that may be damaged

BOTTOMS (PANTS, SKIRTS)

- Hems that may be undone
- Inseams that may be worn out
- Loose buttons
- Stains

SWEATERS

- Holes from pests
- Pulls on the yarn
- Fiber piling
- Stains
- Other

Springtime means not only switching to breezy clothing, but also lightening up on accessories. This means trading out heavy-duty winter leathers for accessories in playful fabrics like straw and linen (or maybe in pastel colors). Here are some general things you can do as you get ready for the seasonal accessory switch. NOTE: *Always check with product care label for specific instructions.*

- For straw hats and bags, you can use a toothbrush or rag with diluted dish soap to gently spot clean any stains. NOTE: Do not soak straw with water. Let air dry.

- For leathers, use a leather cleaning and conditioning product to gently spot clean any stains and restore the luster. If approved by the manufacturer, apply a stain-repellent spray to protect leather from stains.

- Designate a space to store straw items for the season, to keep them within easy reach but protected from being crushed or misshapen. Temporary hooks on a wall or door are a great solution!

SUMMER WARDROBE MAINTENANCE

Summertime is all about outdoor fun and sun-filled escapes. It is probably the season where a minimum wardrobe care effort is desired. It is wearing breezy cottons, sheer voile and other sun-friendly fabrics. It's also about stains from ice cream spills, grass, perspiration and barbecue sauce.

While these stains may be unavoidable, managing them can be easy. The trick is to be prepared when out and about. We recommend "summer-izing" your tote bag or backpack with some essentials to quickly handle pesky wardrobe issues.

SUMMER WARDROBE MAINTENANCE CARE KIT

In a small zippered bag (we suggest a fabric one over a disposable plastic one) pack the following to slip into your carryall:

- Stain treatment wipes or pen
- Fashion tape
- Safety pins (a mini sewing kit)
- A tank top (just in case)
- A change of undies (just in case)
- Hand wipe packets
- Underarm deodorant wipes

NOTE: As always, we suggest following the manufacturer's instruction for care. That being said, most cottons can be safely treated for minor stains on-the-go; plus light hand washing in the stained area.

FALL/WINTER WARDROBE MAINTENANCE

Now is the time to prepare for the colder weather, which means pulling out woolens, heavy knits, leathers and tweeds. Much like spring, it means a major seasonal wardrobe shift.

There are two main objectives with fall maintenance:

1. Just as in spring, do a thorough closet cleaning and revamp in order to evaluate what fall/winter items to keep or shift.

2. Prep your fall wardrobe, in natural and faux hides, for the rigors of wet winter weather (especially boots, purses, snow gear and other accessories).

As in spring, the key idea is to start the season with a fresh look at your closet. Here is a review of those tips and things to keep in mind.

If the task seems daunting, approach it in small sections over the course of a week or so.

- Have a checklist as you go through each garment type to ensure that you are covering the basics.
- Have the tools handy to take care of minor maintenance. More complex repairs can be set aside, so as not to slow down the process of daily maintenance.
- Give items a quick brush to refresh, or set aside to launder if needed.

FALL/WINTER WARDROBE MAINTENANCE CHECKLIST

Give a quick check for the following clothing items.

BLOUSES

- Stains
- Fraying or discoloration on collar
- Snags
- Holes from pests
- Loose buttons
- Embellishments that may be damaged

BOTTOMS (PANTS, SKIRTS)

- Hems that may be undone
- Inseams that may be worn out
- Loose buttons
- Stains

SWEATERS

- Holes from pests
- Pulls on the yarn
- Fiber piling
- Stains
- Other

WET WEATHER PREP (FOR NATURAL AND FAUX HIDES)

Boots and accessories can take a beating during the fall/winter season. There is mess from rain, damage from thawing agents like rock salt, and mud from melting slush.

- Be sure to give a good pre-season prep to jackets and shoes using a leather cleanser and conditioner.
- Use a water-proofing spray to protect leather items. Check manufacturer's label for approval before use.
- Wipe leathers dry as soon as you're out of the rain and snow. But remember to keep them away from heating vents. This can dry the surface and cause cracking.
- Clean residue like rock salt with a damp cloth and leather/suede cleanser soon after coming inside.

VINTAGE CLOTHING CARE

Vintage garments are a wonderful bit of history that connects us to the past, whether it is a special item passed down through generations or an unexpected find in a thrift store.

Caring for these items may require special handling, especially with the cleaning process. For everyday care, here are some suggestions for keeping vintage items in good condition.

STORE IN A FABRIC BAG

For off-season storage, use breathable cotton or muslin bags. These will allow air to circulate inside the bag on a continuous basis. This will minimize stale air from being trapped inside, which can lead to fiber-destroying issues like mold and mildew.

USE THE PROPER HANGER

Never hang stretchable fabrics such as knits. Bias cut fabrics (like chiffon) and heavily-embellished, heavy garments should be put on the proper hanger that can support their weight. This will keep necklines from stretching out and distorting the shape of the garment.

There are specific hangers that are best for certain types of clothing, so be sure to always choose the appropriate one. A sturdy padded hanger is best for gowns and other heavier items, while a thin padded hanger is fine for small tops. When in doubt, store the item flat instead of on a hanger.

PROTECT ITEMS WITH ACID-FREE PAPER

If folding items, use acid-free tissue paper or wrap items in 100% cotton bags. Tissue is also helpful for separating items in a crowded closet or storage box.

Be sure to use tissue to protect embellished items from other items that could snag. Remember to store in a box that allows air to circulate. This keeps stale air trapped in the box from permeating the garments and increased humidity from damaging the fabrics over time.

DEODORIZE GARMENTS SAFELY

Oftentimes, there is a lingering scent if a garment has been purchased from a thrift store. Be sure to clean the item in the most delicate way. A gentle cycle or hand wash is recommended. You may also try deodorizing it in the dryer, with a dryer sheet on low for a few minutes.

HANDLE TRIMS WITH CARE

Vintage garments will most likely have buttons, zippers and other trim that are unique to their era.

If your garment has a metal zipper, for example, it most likely from the early 1960s (or even earlier), as plastic zippers came into popularity in the late 1960s. If it seems hard to open and close, apply a bit of beeswax to keep it running smoothly.

For vintage buttons and other trims, there are sites that specialize in almost any type of items should replacement be necessary.

"The apparel oft proclaims the man.'

—*William Shakespeare*

A CONSCIENTIOUS GUIDE TO WARDROBE CARE

108

GARMENT PRESERVATION

Preserving a garment is a specific process that is different from off-season storage. It is when a garment is put away for the foreseeable future, perhaps to pass it down or enshrine it as a memento of a special occasion.

There are companies that will clean and preserve your garment in a box. If you decide to do it yourself, there are archival and preservation suppliers that sell the boxes designed specifically for storing textiles. Here are some tips:

- It is best to have the garment cleaned by a professional cleaner to remove food stains and other dirt that can damage and discolor fibers over time.
- Store antique textiles flat, with as few folds as possible. If large items must be folded for storage, minimize the number of folds to make sure they do not become permanent creases. Acid-free tissue paper is a great way to stuff sleeves and soften folds.
- Do not hang antique garments; flat storage is best.
- Store textiles in a cool, dry location. Avoid using trunks or boxes in hot attics or in damp basements or garages. Damp conditions can encourage the growth of mold as well as attract insects.
- Make sure your hands are clean, or wear gloves, when preserving garments, to avoid transfer of oils and other elements that may affect the fibers over time.

MENDING

With the modern busy lifestyle, it seems quaint and old-fashioned to darn socks and repair holes in a garment. Add to this the availability of inexpensive clothing, and it seems a better use of valuable time to throw something out rather than repair it. Why spend time fixing a $30 top, when it is easier to replace it? Thinking about sending it to the cleaners for repair? The cost may be close to the price of buying a new one, in this case.

Times have changed, however, as we begin to understand the ecological crisis we face by throwing away clothing. There are several positives to mending. There is a sense of pride in keeping something for as long as possible. You are lessening your negative environmental impact with the sustainable practice of mending rather than throwing items out. It is ultimately cheaper! A few moments mending something means spending less money on new clothing. Perhaps limiting the opportunities to impulse buy. It is one way to reinforce value in the clothing you purchase.

Like anything, mending is an art. One that goes beyond sewing on a loose button or tacking up a hem. The intricacies of mending stitches are beyond the scope of this book. But we do offer some ideas and a list of basic tools.

APPLY A PATCH

Layering a piece of fabric or decorative decal over a rip or per-manent stain is a great opportunity to give new life to a damaged fashion favorite.

A similar colored fabric square can create a blended look. Artfully designed patches or embellishments such as lace, studs, rhine-stones, etc. can really create a unique look. Check out your local fab-ric store for interesting patches that can be sewn or ironed on in a pinch. Online resources may also offer options, from vintage to themed patches.

USE DECORATIVE STITCHES

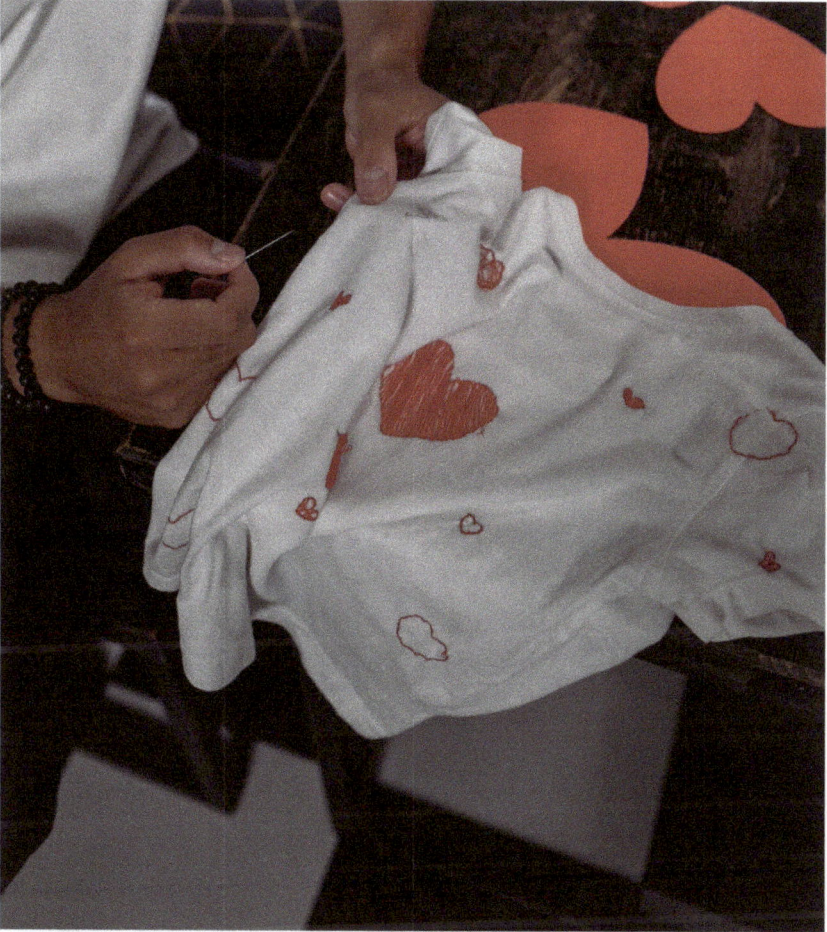

Repairing a sizable rip can involve fancy hand needlework such as cross stitches, blanket stitches and running stitches. These can create a decorative look to the outside of the garment by embracing the tear rather than trying to hide it, turning what was an accidental hole into a work of art!

Some expertise is needed to master these types of handwork. Some programmable sewing machines can do the work for you.

ADD A DECONSTRUCTED LOOK

Getting an accidental rip in your favorite denim shirt or jeans doesn't mean the end. The deconstructed look can be found in denim at every price level. It's that torn, worn and shredded look that creates a street-wise edge.

If embracing this look, care should be taken to reinforce the back of that area, with fusible interfacing or some other adherent, to make sure that the tear is confined. Some stitching may also be needed to keep the fray from spreading during the wash cycle.

DYE THE GARMENT

This is not a sewing technique, but it is a way to rejuvenate a garment that is looking worn or has stains.

Dyeing has come a long way from the simple techniques with familiar drug store brands. There is now a plethora of modern kits that offer endless possibilities. From dyeing your garments in a wide range of fashionable solid colors to sophisticated, trendy techniques (Shibori, ombre, etc). So even a beginner can produce boutique-level results.

It is well worth researching the opportunity to have some fun with creating a unique, work-of-art garment through dyeing techniques.

MENDING TOOLS

Here is a list of some basic things to add to your sewing kit for doing specialized mending repairs.

- Darning mushroom (to stabilize small areas being worked on)
- Embroidery loop (for larger work areas on a garment)
- Darning needles
- Assortment of patches (denim, leather, lace, etc.)
- Embroidery thread
- Fusible backing (to stabilize a tear from the underside)
- Double sided fusible (to attach fabric or patch that has no adhesive)
- Anti-fray liquid or spray
- Knitting or crochet needle to pull thread through (for knits)

"I see that the fashion wears out more apparel than the man."

—William Shakespeare

BASIC CARE FOR
FABRIC TYPES

These are some general rules of thumb for wardrobe care based on the fabric. Since there might be specific considerations due to trims and other details, we do recommend deferring to the manufacturer's instruction as the primary source of care.

The fabric care guide is categorized by fabrics

- Cotton Care Tips
- Leather Care Tips
- Linen Care Tips
- Fur Care Tips
- Wool Care Tips
- Knit Care Tips
- Delicate Fabric Care Tips (lace, organza, chiffon, satin, etc)

COTTON CARE TIPS

- Natural fabrics, like cotton, tend to lose color during the wash more so than polyester. So be sure to wash similar cotton colors together.
- To minimize wrinkling from the wash, remove cottons from the dryer while still slightly damp and hang to completely dry.
- If recommended, using a light wisp of spray starch and ironing items will keep cottons looking crisp and fresh during multiple wears.
- Cotton is known for being prone to wrinkles. If that is a concern, check if the label says that the cotton has been treated with a wrinkle resistant finish.
- Items like cotton T-shirts and jeans often don't need ironing if you gently stretch them when they come out of the washing machine and then air dry them flat. Also use the 'reduced creases' setting on your washing machine if available.
- 100% cotton (which is plant based) will not attract clothing moths. If it is combined with animal fibers (e.g. silk) it may become susceptible to moth damage. Animal fibers contain keratin, a natural protein that larvae feed upon, creating damaging holes in these clothing items.
  - Be sure to clean these items regularly to remove possible larvae.
  - Store with moth repellent off-season.

LINEN CARE TIPS

- Most linens can be hand washed or gently machine washed and hung dry (which can save on dry cleaning costs). But please check with care label before proceeding!
- If linens can be washed, remove from the dryer when still slightly damp to avoid the linen becoming stiff, and hang or lie flat to finish off the drying process.
- Store in a breathable bag to allow air to circulate. This reduces the opportunity for mold and mildew to form (particularly during off-season storage).
- 100% linen (which is plant based) will not attract clothing moths. If it is combined with animal fibers (e.g. silk) it may become susceptible to moth damage. Animal fibers contain keratin, a natural protein that larvae feed upon, creating damaging holes in these clothing items.
  - Be sure to clean these items regularly to remove possible larvae.
  - Store with moth repellent off-season
- Be careful with the oils from moth repellents and other protective products. If they come into direct contact with your wardrobe item over a long period of time they can cause damage.

LEATHER CARE TIPS

- Most leather is sturdy but it's best not to store items near extreme heat (e.g. ventilators). This can dry and crack the fabric.
- If recommended, use a leather conditioner to keep items supple and clean.
- Store in a breathable bag to allow air to circulate. This reduces the opportunity for mold and mildew to form (particularly during off-season storage).
- If recommended, use a spray guard on the leather before wear. This will help to protect it against water marks, stains and dirt.
- If the leather gets wet, wipe water away and air dry in room temperature setting (not extreme heat or cold).
- Just as leather shoes stretch, so do leather garments. Use appropriate hangers that can support the weight and shape of the garment. Do not hang leather garments on pegs or hooks that can cause them to become misshapen.

KNIT CARE TIPS

- Check knits periodically for loose fibers and use a de-fuzzer to remove balls of pilled fibers from the surface of the knit. A crochet needle makes easy work of guiding snagged fibers to the inside of the sweater.
- Launder sweater inside out. This helps to reduce friction (and thus wear and tear) to the outside surface during the wash cycle.
- Using a wash bag is also a great way to keep knits safe from wear and tear during the machine wash cycle.
- Follow laundering instructions for the best results. In general, hand-washing or gentle machine washing with a mild soap is best. Air drying is preferred to keep sweaters from shrinking, or to prevent damage to the fibers.
- Store sweaters flat. This keeps them from stretching out of shape, and is particularly important for loosely woven knits.

WOOL CARE TIPS

- As mentioned previously, woolens (which are animal based) contain keratin. This is a natural protein that larvae feed upon, creating damaging holes in these clothing items.
  - Be sure to clean these items regularly to remove possible larvae.
  - Store with moth repellent off season.
- Be sure to air out after wearing. Pests are not just attracted to the fibers but also to the smell of food residue, body oils, perfumes and other odors that may linger.
- As with any other garments, be sure to clean for end-of-season storage. Air tight, plastic containers can be used but be sure to store them in settings that are not too hot or cold. Breathable, cotton containers are more highly recommended to keep woolens safe for storage.
- Periodically vacuum and refresh areas in your closet, especially those in which woolens and furs are kept.
- Be careful with the oils from moth repellents and other protective products. If they come into direct contact with your wardrobe item over a long period of time they can cause damage.

FAUX FUR CARE TIPS

- Periodically use a brush with widely spaced bristles (like a pet hair slicker brush) to gently remove food particles and dust that may be trapped in the fibers. This is better than a lint brush, which can stick to fiber. Be sure to brush with the nap of the fur.

- Store in a breathable bag to allow air to circulate. This reduces the opportunity for mold and mildew to form (particularly during off-season storage).

- Check areas often where oil from the skin and dirt can accumulate (neckline and cuff). If recommended, spot clean to keep these from damaging the nap.

- If fur gets wet, it is best to air dry (if using a dryer is recommended by the manufacturer, then that is okay).

DELICATE FABRIC CARE TIPS (LACE, ORGANZA, CHIFFON, SATIN, ETC)

- Be sure to use a padded hanger that is appropriate to the weight of the item (e.g. a full-length negligee may need a heavy-duty padded hanger, while a lightly embellished top may do fine on a thin velvet hanger).
- Consider flat storage for long-term needs to avoid stress on the fiber, and to keep the garment from stretching at the neckline.
- Whether storing hung or flat, it is a good idea to keep these items inside a breathable bag to avoid snags and to reduce the opportunity for mold and mildew to form (particularly during off-season storage).
- If fabrics are washable:
  - Place inside a wash bag at the most delicate setting to avoid wear and tear in the machine.
  - Make sure that all closures are done up to avoid snaps and zippers from snagging onto the delicate fabric during the wash cycle.
- Always check the manufacturer label to see ironing instructions.
- An alternative to ironing may be to hang the item in a steam-filled bathroom or use a steaming device (held at least 6" away with constant motion) to loosen wrinkles.

*"Clothes make the man. Naked people have little or
no influence on society."*

—Mark Twain

PART 4 - THE TOOLS

There are a myriad of wardrobe organizing methodologies. Whatever works best for your needs and space is great!

Our Wardrobe Care Tip Guide is more about care and maintenance, with basic ideas and principles that apply for any organizing techniques.

We want to make things easy, so we have designed this part of the guide into pages that can be copied, or cut out and hung in your closet, dressing area and laundry room for quick reference.

- Wardrobe Care Tool Kit (home, vacation, kids and more)
- Stain Treatment Tips (feel free to edit and add your own hacks)
- Quick Daily Wardrobe Maintenance Tips

WARDROBE CARE TOOL KIT

The easiest way to keep your wardrobe in shape is to have the tools at hand to handle quick repairs and perform maintenance as needed.

- Sewing kit
- Sweater fuzz remover
- Small scissors
- Stain wipes
- Lint brush
- Fabric brush
- Seam ripper (great for removing garment tags that itch)
- Suede cleaner
- Fusible Bonding Web (no-sew repair for hems and opened seams)
- Fusing web (to repair small fabric rips from behind)
- Water repellent spray
- Leather cleaner
- Suede brush
- Soft cloth to clean leather
- Metal polish/cleaner (for hardware like buckles, studs, etc.)
- Fashion tape
- Button/trim container (for extra buttons, etc. that come with outfits)
- Care instructions (if they come with an outfit or accessory)
- Crochet needle (to pull sweater snags through)
- Shoe care kit
- Steamer (hand held is convenient)
- _____
- _____
- _____
- _____

This page is left intentionally blank, so you
can cut out this Tool Guide for handy reference and to keep within easy reach.

VACATION WARDROBE CARE KIT

Be prepared for fashion emergencies when you are away from home (and without the ability to pull a change of outfit from your closet). These are the essentials that you can put into a small zippered pouch, to slip into your luggage. There is also room for your own ideas.

As always, we recommend checking with the care label before laundering any garment.

- Stain wipes (a pen or packets) for a quick dab of the stains.
- Travel sewing kit. The alternative is to create one with a threaded needle stuck through a 3×5 card (or other thick paper) plus a few safety pins. Fold the paper over to create a match book type closure and secure with a piece of tape.
- Fashion tape. These are great for hems and small tears. You can purchase these in multi packs. Just toss a few into your kit and replace as needed.
- A pair of undies. A thong or bikini style that will be less bulky in a small bag is best.
- A tank top or tee shirt (in case the spill warrants a change).
- Zipper repair kit (NOTE: some require tools like wire snips and pliers but a pair of scissors may do in a pinch)
- _____
- _____
- _____
- _____

This page is left intentionally blank, so you
can cut out this Tool Guide for handy reference and to keep within easy reach.

KIDS WARDROBE CARE KIT

Stains and kids seem to go hand in hand. With lots of active play and unexpected oops, it can give parents and caregivers some peace of mind to be ready for (almost) anything.

As always, we recommend checking with the care label before laundering any garment. Here is a list of some ideas. Plus room to add your own ideas.

- Stain wipes
- General hand and body wipes
- Change of clothing (leggings or knit pants and a long sleeve top that rolls compactly into the bag is best.
- Underwear
- Shoes or sandals (if you've ever had a child have a mishap that went all the way to their shoes, you'll be glad you did)
- Plastic bag for soiled items
- Sewing Kit
- Extra bib (for babies and toddlers)
- Scrunchies
- _____
- _____
- _____
- _____

This page is left intentionally blank, so you can cut out this Tool Guide for handy reference and to keep within easy reach.

SPECIAL EVENT WARDROBE CARE KIT

Being away from home with a special occasion outfit can be a little stressful. What if something goes wrong with it? There is no way to simply run to your closet for an alternative nor opt for another ensemble (if you are part of a coordinated group). Being ready for "worst-case scenario" helps.

While there are convenient, ready-made kits for all kinds of occasions (weddings, galas, proms, etc.) we think a great option is to create a kit from items you might already have. This way, you can customize your kit to the essentials that you need, and replenish items for future events.

As always, we recommend checking with the care label before laundering any garment. Here is a list of some ideas you can put in a small zippered pouch. Plus, room to add your own.

- Stain wipes (a pen or packets) for a quick dab of the stains.
- Travel sewing kit. The alternative is to create one with a threaded needle stuck through a 3×5 card (or other thick paper) plus a few safety pins. Fold the paper over to create a match book type closure and secure with a piece of tape.
- Fashion tape. These are great for hems and small tears.
- Ironing cloth (for protecting your attire from scorching if a quick touch up is need. Ideal for velvet or other delicate fabrics).
- Zipper repair kit (NOTE: some require tools like wire snips and pliers but a pair of scissors may do in a pinch).
- Sandals in a neutral shade or close to your outfit color (in case your wardrobe malfunction involves your shoes breaking).
- _____
- _____
- _____
- _____

This page is left intentionally blank, so you can cut out this Tool Guide for handy reference and to keep within easy reach.

EVERY DAY WARDROBE CARE KIT

As you go about your day, sometimes there is a need for a quick wardrobe fix. Typically, you'd want a kit that can fit easily into a small purse, tote bag or backpack.

As mentioned before, there are pre-made kits that cover most fashion emergencies. We think a great option is to create a kit from items that you might already have. This way you can customize your kit to the essentials you need, and replenish as necessary. Here are some ideas for items you can put into a small zippered pouch (maybe even a coin change purse or credit card holder!).

- Stain wipes (one or two packets) for a quick dab of the stains.
- Fashion tape. These are great for hems and small tears. You can purchase these in multi packs. Just toss a few into your kit and replace as needed.
- Travel sewing kit. The alternative is to create one with a threaded needle stuck through a 3×5 card (or other thick paper) plus a few safety pins. Fold the paper over to create a match book type closure and secure with a piece of tape.
- _____
- _____
- _____
- _____

This page is left intentionally blank, so you can cut out this Tool Guide for handy reference and to keep within easy reach.

OUTDOOR ACTIVITY WARDROBE CARE KIT

For outdoor trips (hiking, camping, etc.), a minor wardrobe malfunction might not be a priority, but it can be more than a nuisance if the article of clothing is an important part of your gear.

So what is important to carry with you? It depends. A local day hike may not require anything at all. However, a week-long trek through harsh conditions or unfamiliar terrain may necessitate more careful wardrobe care considerations. Also, if you are carrying lots of gear, you probably want to keep things as light as possible.

The good news? Many of the recommended items are available in super slim, compact travel size versions, so they will not add weight to your gear. You will, however, be so relieved that you have them, if needed! Here are our suggestions, and room to add your own ideas.

- Travel sewing kit. The alternative is to create one with a threaded needle stuck through a 3×5 card (or other thick paper) plus a few safety pins. Fold the paper over to create a match book type closure and secure with a piece of tape.
- Duct Tape (A classic! It may not be pretty, but it can cover large tears in a jacket, gloves or other items).
- Stain wipes
- Stop Fray glue (great for holding fabric edges or ripped seams that may shred while wearing).
- Water repellent spray (check with care label to ensure it is safe for the fabric)
- Repair patches for fabrics (peel and stick)
- Zipper repair kit (NOTE: some require tools like wire snips and pliers but a pair of scissors may do in a pinch)
- _____
- _____
- _____
- _____

This page is left intentionally blank, so you
can cut out this Tool Guide for handy reference and to keep within easy reach.

ADDITIONAL TIPS ABOUT WARDROBE CARE TOOLS

We have provided some basic lists for creating a variety of wardrobe care tool kits. In this section, we offer some additional ideas that may be helpful in this task.

Sewing Tools

- If you choose to create your own sewing kit, opt for medium size needles. These needles are easier to thread and versatile enough to work with a variety of fabrics (from cottons to heavier denims and satin).
- Choose high-quality threads that won't break easily after the repair is made.
- A pack of clear buttons is indispensable in your wardrobe care kit. If you lose a button in a conspicuous location, replace it with one from a less conspicuous area; and temporarily replace that one with a clear button.

Laundry Tools

There are a myriad of hacks and techniques for getting out stains. Our main tip is to have a variety of tools in your arsenal for laundry day, to make the task of clothing care a bit easier. As always, we recommend making sure that cleansers and pre-treatment products are okay for a particular fabric before use. Here are some basic needs.

- A heavy duty laundry detergent for tough stains
- A gentle soap for knits and other delicate items
- Laundry soap bar (optional for hand washing items)
- Fabric softener
- Baking soda (a classic pre-treatment product for stains)
- Toothbrush (to add a little extra scrub on tough stains with a pre-treatment product)

- Dryer sheets to remover static cling build up.
- Stain treatment spray
- Bleach
- Mesh bags to wash delicate items
- Hand held steamer
- A small basin or tub for soaking items, if necessary

TRAVEL TOOLS

- Be aware of on-boarding regulations for sharp objects (scissors, etc.) in your carry-on. If you have check-in luggage, consider leaving them in those bags.
- Most pre-made sewing kits come with basic thread colors. If your event outfit is an unusual color, add a small spool to match.
- Consider the type of garments you will be wearing, and also your destination. Pack your kit accordingly (e.g. you may not need the leather repair kit if you are going for summer vacation to a beach in Cancun).
- Some hotels may supply you with a sewing kit, if needed. But we always recommend being prepared: mishaps can occur anywhere; the hotel may not have a sewing kit available; or you may be under a rushed timeframe to handle fashion emergencies.
- For hand washing a stained garment, in a pinch, opt for the hotel shampoo rather than the bath bar soap (which can actually set the stain). Just make sure it is not a combo shampoo and conditioner.
- The hotel hair dryer is tempting to use for quickly drying a garment. Be aware that heat can also set stains and damage delicate fabrics. Check with the care label for the best approach.

- If the label approves putting the garment in the dryer at home, go ahead and use the blow dryer heat sparingly. Keep it well away from direct contact with the fabric.
- If the label says tumble dry low or no heat, use a cold setting on the blow dryer and keep it well away from direct contact with the fabric.
- Hang drying is the best recommendation if unsure and if there is time to do so.

- A coin purse or credit card holder makes a great container for everyday wardrobe care items. They easily fit packet-size stain wipes and a DIY sewing kit; and are compact enough to slip neatly into small handbags or backpacks.

AT-HOME GARMENT TRY-ON TOOLS

Trying on an outfit (whether for everyday or a special occasion need) is not generally in the category of wardrobe care. It is important though, to make sure that you are judging the outfit under the optimum condition. It is amazing what adding a few accessories can do to improve the look and feel of a garment being tried on!

Taking these steps will hopefully reduce the chance of returns. Thus saving time, money and resources associated with the return process. If the outfit looks fine, that's great! If you love it but it needs tailoring, make a note of those areas of concern. It will help to make the process easier when meeting with the tailor. Here are some things to have on hand, if applicable.

Women

- Shape wear (to help the garment fall correctly). This can make a huge difference in how it looks!
- Proper shoes

- Appropriate undergarment (bra, undies, slip, etc.)
- Jewelry
- Other accessories (hat, scarf, purse, etc.)
- Hair accessories and clips (if you plan an up-do, to try to simulate the look)
- Makeup guard (to protect the garment from accidental makeup and hair product smudges)

Men

- Shirt (button down or tee shirt, whichever is planned for the ensemble)
- Tie
- Belt
- Proper shoes
- Other accessories (hat, etc.)
- Jewelry

STAIN TREATMENT TIPS

Suggested treatments are for non fading, washable fabrics. Check care instructions before trying anything.

BLOOD

Soak in cold water to remove as much of the stain as possible. Blot (do not rub) with a stain remover (hydrogen peroxide also works great) and launder as usual.

BODY STAINS (SWEAT, COLLAR/CUFF SOIL, DEODORANT)

Blot (do not rub) with a stain remover. Soak in a mixture of warm water and mild detergent for 15-30 minutes. Launder as usual.

COFFEE/TEA

Blot (do not rub) with a stain remover. Soak in a mixture of mild soap (detergent, not bar soap) and cold water for 10-20 minutes. Launder as usual.

CANDLE WAX

Remove the dried wax with a dull knife or card. Place stain side down between white paper towels and press with a slightly warm iron until no more stain transfers. Change paper towels often. Apply a spot remover, hand wash in warm soapy water. Rinse and hang dry.

CHEWING GUM

Apply ice to harden the stain. Scrape carefully with an object with a dull edge (e.g. spoon, plastic card). Blot (do not rub) with stain remover. Launder as usual.

DRINKS (BEER, FRUIT JUICE, SODA, BERRIES)

If stain is fresh, rinse with cold water. Soak item in a solution of mild soap (detergent, not bar soap) and cold water for 15-30 minutes. Launder.

FELT TIP PEN

On colorfast washables, Soak for 10 minutes in a mixture of non-chlorine soap and a few drops of **ammonia**. Rinse and then launder as usual. Some felt markers will leave a permanent stain.

GRAVIES/SAUCES, ICE CREAM

Treat with stain remover. Rinse with cold water. If stain persists, soak garment in mild detergent and cold water for 15-30 minutes. Launder as usual.

GREASE (OIL, BUTTER, DRESSING, ETC)

Use stain remover and launder as usual. If stain remains, sprinkle with cornstarch or unmedicated talc powder. Let stand for 5-10 minutes. Repeat.

LIPSTICK/MAKEUP (FOR COLORFAST WASHABLES)

If stain is fresh, use stain remover and launder. If dried, try blotting with rubbing alcohol. Immediately rinse and launder as recommended.

INK /BALLPOINT

For colorfast washables, spray with aerosol hairspray. Launder in cold water as usual. Repeat if necessary.

NAIL POLISH

Place stain down over paper towels. Carefully sponge with

acetone for 10-15 minutes. Rinse in cold water and launder. Acetone can damage some fabrics. Do not use on DYNEL, ACETATE or SPANDEX.

WINE (RED OR WHITE)

If stain is wet, saturate with club soda and blot (do not rub) with a clean towel. Wash in cold water with detergent (not a bar soap). Rinse and hang dry.

QUICK DAILY WARDROBE MAINTENANCE TIPS

Got just a few minutes to do a quick wardrobe maintenance? Here's what you can do within these time frames. You will be surprised at how much you can get done.

PREPARATION

- First you will need a timer to make sure you don't go over.
- Next, do a one time gathering of Wardrobe Care Tools you may need (see our suggested list in the guide)

PICK YOUR BEST SOLUTION

2-MINUTE WARDROBE CARE

- Organize a few things (put on hanger, straighten, fold in drawer, etc)
- De-clutter by putting one item in the donate/resell/repair basket
- Run a brush over a few hanging tops and bottoms to pick up any food particles or other detritus that may be stuck in fibers (and that can attract pests).

5-MINUTE WARDROBE CARE

- Organize a few things (put on hanger, straighten, fold in drawer, etc)
- De-clutter by putting one item in the donate/resell/repair basket
- Run a brush over a few hanging tops and bottoms to pick up any food particles or other detritus that may be stuck in fibers (and that can attract pests).
- Do a quick wipe or buff a pair of shoes, purse, belt buckle)

10-MINUTE WARDROBE CARE

- Organize a few things (put on hanger, straighten, fold in drawer, etc)
- De-clutter by putting one item in the donate/resell/repair basket
- Run a brush over a few hanging tops and bottoms to pick up any food particles or other detritus that may be stuck in fibers (and that can attract pests).
- Do a quick wipe or buff a pair of shoes, purse, belt buckle)
- Put away some laundry

IN CONCLUSION

We hope we have been informative with this book, by shining a light on the environmental concerns surrounding the practice of dumping clothing into landfills. And perhaps we've inspired you to take action, with practical steps to help minimize or prevent your fashion favorites from adding to this environmental problem.

We know the magnitude of the issue can seem daunting. Can saving one piece of clothing from a landfill truly make any difference? Think about it this way. If one million people, for example, each saved even a single tee shirt from being thrown away, that's one million fewer tee shirts being added to landfills.

Our efforts, in this regard, has a cumulative effect. On a global scale, it becomes one area in which we can help to fight the environmental issues that are threatening the safety of our planet.

ABOUT THE AUTHOR

Sheryll Fraze has loved the creative arts and clothing from a very young age.

She has been in the fashion business for over 30 years: first as a designer in Manhattan's 7th Avenue garment district, after graduating from the prestigious Fashion Institute of Technology; then in various positions in California, where she now resides. These included being a retail store manager, merchandiser and buyer. She credits her experiences on both the wholesale and retail sides of the fashion business with giving her broad expertise about fashion and its ecological impact. These insights were the inspiration to write this book. Her company Garment Saver has been in business over 15 years, helping clients care for their wardrobe with eco-friendly organizers and protectors for home storage and travel needs.

REFERENCE SOURCES

https://www.trunkclub.com/press/news/packing-its-not-as-easy-as-you-think. Accessed 3/1/2022

smithsonianmag.com/smart-news/case-washing-clothes-cold-water. Accessed 3/1/2022

https://www.cnbc.com/2019/01/10/growing-online-sales-means-more-returns-and-trash-for-landfills.html. Accessed 3/1/2022

https://fashinza.com/textile/design-trends/african-fashion-fashion-weeks-in-africa/

https://www.harpersbazaar.com/culture/features/a43521481/fast-fashion-quality/?utm_source=pocket-newtab

https://www.abc.net.au/news/2021-08-12/fast-fashion-turning-parts-ghana-into-toxic-land-fill/100358702

https://www.epa.gov/facts-and-figures-about-materials-waste-and-recycling/textiles-material-specific-data

https://imperfectidealist.com/where-to-donate-clothes-besides-goodwill/. Accessed 3/1/2022

https://www.weforum.org/projects/circular-economy. Accessed 3/1/2022

https://www.archives.gov/publications/prologue/2016/summer/preserve-textiles.html. Accessed 3/20/2022

https://www.uhcsafetrip.com/tips/traveling-light-how-to-streamline-while-packing/. Accessed 3/20/2022

https://www.vogue.com/article/caring-for-vintage-clothing-tips.Accessed 3/21/2022

thespruce.com/why-clothes-shrink-in-the-laundry. Accessed 3/21/2022

https://www.kshs.org/p/preserving-textiles/12266. Accessed 3/21/2022

https://www.charliesoap.com/how-to-remove-salt-stains-from-boots-and-winter-clothes/https://www.loveyourclothes.org.uk/guides/how-care-cotton. Accessed 3/25/2022

https://www.modernretail.co/retailers/why-childrens-apparel-growth-is-outpacing-mens-and-womens-wear/ Accessed 4/1/2022

https://www.comscore.com/por/Insights/Blog/Apparel-Spending-Shifting-to-Online-Channels-Faster-than-Total-Retail-Dollars. Accessed 4/10/2022

https://www.ramseysolutions.com/budgeting/stop-impulse-buys. Accessed 4/10/2022

https://www.roadrunnerwm.com/blog/textile-waste-environmental-crisis. Accessed 5/14/2022

https://www.thespruce.com/insects-that-eat-holes-in-clothes-2146424. Accessed 5/14/2022

megaclothespegs.com. Accessed 5/10/2022

https://www.nylon.com/sequins-glitter-are-bad-environment. Accessed 5/15/2022

totalwardrobecare.co.uk/blog/what-materials-do-moths-eat/. Accessed 5/15/2022

walthamservices.com/blog/silverfish-control/do-silverfish-eat-clothes/. Accessed 6/5/2022

https://fashinnovation.nyc/fashion-industry-statistics/. Accessed 10/6/2022

https://www.roadrunnerwm.com/blog/textile-waste-environmental-crisis Accessed 10/6/2022

https://www.projectcece.com/blog/506/how-many-times-do-we-wear-our-clothes/. Accessed 10/6/2022

https://www.lcca.org.uk/blog/fashion/the-impact-of-bloggers-and-influencers-on-the-fashion-industry/. Accessed 10/6/2022

https://www.forbes.com/sites/catherineerdly/2021/06/27/the-resale-market-is-booming-heres-how-small-businesses-can-benefit/?sh=2e2087be7c62. Accessed 10/6/2022

https://www.usnews.com/news/best-countries/articles/2021-11-11/how-dead-white-mans-clothing-is-clogging-the-global-south. Accessed 10/6/2022

https://www.triplepundit.com/story/2016/quenching-cottons-thirst-reducing-use-water-cotton-lifecycle/57196. Accessed 10/6/2022

https://www.theguardian.com/fashion/2020/sep/20/the-rise-of-fashion-rental-scarlett-conlon. Accessed 10/6/2022

https://www.elle.com/uk/fashion/trends/a36282440/upcycling-clothes/. Accessed 10/6/2022

https://www.thebalancesmb.com/the-basics-of-recycling-clothing-and-other-textiles-2877780. Accessed 10/6/2022

https://www.fallsgarden.com/plants-used-for-clothing/. Accessed 10/6/2022

nyorganicdrycleaners.com/laundry-101-what-causes-clothes-to-fade/. Accessed 10/6/2022

hunker.com/13416415/what-causes-mold-in-the-closet. Accessed 10/6/2022

https://www.leathercult.com/blog/why-leather-jacket-cracks-and-how-to-prevent-it/ Accessed 10/6/2022

https://tide.com/en-us/how-to-wash-clothes/washing-different-fabrics-and-colors. Accessed 10/6/2022

https://theprettyplaneteer.com/cost-per-wear-the-true-cost-of-your-clothes/. Accessed 10/6/2022

www.cleanipedia.com. Accessed 10/6/2022

https://www.brainyquote.com/topics/clothes-quotes. Accessed 10/6/2022

https://www.epa.gov/assessing-and-managing-chemicals-under-tsca/final-risk-evaluation-perchloroethylene#findings. Accessed 10/6/2022

PHOTO CREDIT – PEXELS.COM

We graciously acknowledge the photographers on Pexel.com; whose images were used throughout the book.
pexels-anete-lusina-4792063
pexels-thevibrantmachine-3045624
pexels-татьяна-танатова-4153098
pexels-cottonbro-6865186
pexels-lara-jameson-9324375
pexels-markus-winkler-3812433
pexels-teona-swift-6851281
pexels-katie-rainbow-8317887
pexels-ron-lach-9985942
pexels-rafael-randy-cardoso-garcia-10811537
pexels-animesh-srivastava-8515487
pexels-anete-lusina-4792063
pexels-matt-hardy-2658451
pexels-pavel-danilyuk-7406066
pexels-mart-production-7679682
pexels-sam-lion-5709631
pexels-monica-turlui-7851632
pexels-dmitriy-ganin-7789141
pexels-aleksey-danilov-12267652
pexels-greengrey-darya-11541395
pexels-cottonbro-3206080
pexels-polina-tankilevitch-6630903
pexels-ashley-esakin-10770964
pexels-cottonbro-6865186
pexels-burcu-koleli-3918426
pexels-karolina-grabowska-5202797
pexels-liza-summer-6347525
pexels-ron-lach-9594415
pexels-cottonbro-3662839
pexels-timur-weber-9186164
pexels-anna-shvets-4482900
pexels-vie-studio-6168221
pexels-sam-lion-5709614
pexels-sam-lion-5709631
pexels-mart-production-7679791
pexels-ron-lach-9594415
pexels-artem-podrez-7048262
pexels-cottonbro-studio-6764700
pexels-leticia-ribeiro-2249249
pexels-anastasia-shuraeva-5705493
pexels-anete-lusina-7256911
pexels-sandra-seitamaa-9701372
pexels-timur-weber-9186174
pexels-erik-karits-6526933
pexels-ron-lach-8387124
pexels-los-muertos-crew-8030160
pexels-liza-summer-6347879
pexels-muhammad-amdad-hossain-12070142
pexels-burcu-koleli-3918426
pexels-rachel-claire-6123224

"I wasn't really naked. I simply didn't have any clothes on."

—Josephine Baker

www.ingramcontent.com/pod-product-compliance
Lightning Source LLC
Chambersburg PA
CBHW072147270326
41931CB00010B/1918